GREAT STOCK CAR RACES

Triumphs & Tragedies of Yesterday & Today

Glenda J. Fordham

OVER
TIME
BOOKS

The Publisher: Overtime Books is an imprint of Éditions de
  la Montagne Verte

Library and Archives Canada Cataloguing in Publication

Fordham, Glenda J., 1953–
  Greatest stock car races : triumphs & tragedies of yesterday &
today / Glenda J. Fordham.

  Includes bibliographical references.
  ISBN-13: 978-1-897277-05-8
  ISBN-10: 1-897277-05-9

  1. Stock car racing—United States—History. I. Title.

GV1029.9.S74F67 2006   796.720973   C2006-901847-2

Project Director: J. Alexander Poulton

Cover Image: Courtesy of Corbis, George Tiedemann, photographer,
NewSport

PC:P5

Dedication

To Jacqui, whose friendship and support
helped fuel my creative drive to share
my love of stock car racing

Contents

Acknowledgments

Special thanks to Mario Andretti for generously sharing his thoughts and memories; Brad Moran of Barrie Speedway for his hospitality and sharing his vast knowledge of stock car racing; Allan & Michael Gold for their invaluable first-hand accounts of driving; Laura Lang and Greg MacPherson of *Inside Track Magazine* for their kind assistance with contacts and historical background; Deborah and Brent for resuscitating a dead hard-drive—the best pit crew a writer ever had; Irene Trester for encouragement and numerous encouraging kicks in my rear bumper; Jeff Gordon for bringing me to stock car racing and Greg Biffle for keeping me in the family.

Introduction

Stock car racing's roots go way back to the Prohibition era of the 1920s and early 1930s, when the secret distilling of whiskey or "moonshine" was rampant, especially in the southeastern United States. Transporting the illegal hooch from hidden stills was a dangerous activity. The local bootleggers ran deliveries across state lines at high speeds, mostly at night, with the police and government "revenuers" in hot pursuit. Moonshine running was not only the inspiration for TV's *Dukes of Hazzard* and Burt Reynold's numerous *Smokey and the Bandit* movies, but also for what we now know as stock car racing. Sounds romantic and exciting but back then, the penalty for losing these "races" was loss of income or worse—prison.

As the moonshine business grew, so did the fame of the drivers on the secret Sunday night booze runs. The whiskey runners started racing each other to see who had the fastest cars or who could turn corners the tightest. Bootleggers held these races on Sunday afternoons then drove the same cars to haul cases of moonshine that night. Word quietly leaked out about the racing, and folks came out and lined the back roads to watch. Moonshine car racing became popular in the South—watching was free, and there was little entertainment available during the Depression era in rural areas. Because of the huge tax placed on whiskey after the Volstead Act was repealed in 1933, bootlegging continued for several years after the end of Prohibition.

In one of those perfectly timed moments, William H.G. "Bill" France organized a race on the sands of Daytona Beach, Florida, in the summer of 1938. France had realized the overwhelming popularity of the moonshine runners' races was not going away. Audiences were growing, and gambling and wagering replaced the excitement of the once-illicit booze. He launched a series of races the following summer on the firm, wide sands of Daytona, and the winners of these early organized races received modest prizes such as a box of cigars, bottles of rum and whiskey as well as cases of motor oil.

Bill France became the visionary who realized the potential in developing an official organization that would oversee the races, enforce safety rules, keep records of race champions and statistics and create a peripheral revenue source for himself and his driver teams. However, with the onset of World War II, stock car racing ceased because of the shortage of fuel and materials for rebuilding smashed cars—and, of course, the lack of drivers, who had either enlisted or been drafted. As the war ended and drivers returned, some of the drivers ran the odd race at places like the beach at Daytona.

But in 1947, France realized the time was right to introduce a national sanctioning organization to govern this new sport of stock car racing. In December of that same year, he invited local and out-of-state promoters to Daytona, where they drafted a set of rules and agreed to track specifications over the course of three days. They named the organization the National Association for Stock Car Auto Racing. And so NASCAR was born.

Over the years, stock car racing has become one of the biggest spectator sports in North America, and the sport is currently gaining fans overseas as well as north and south of the U.S. borders. Huge speedway tracks have been built to accommodate over 100,000 fans, and TV broadcast deals have been inked in the hundreds of millions of dollars. Corporate sponsorship has allowed owners to run more than one car; each Busch or Nextel Cup Series vehicle currently costs in the region of $5–7 million per year, not including driver fees.

The Canadian regulating body (CASCAR) is currently expanding its race series, gaining fans and attracting corporate interests. Many CASCAR Super Series races are broadcast on the same sports networks as "big brother" NASCAR. Canadian Indy star Paul Tracy has shown great interest in exploring stock car competition, and in 2006, he will be catching some rides on the NASCAR circuit.

But with all of the money and exposure, it's still the pure excitement at the trackside that gets fans' hearts pounding. The near misses, the big wrecks, the bumper-to-bumper racing for the checkered flag and the glory of Victory Lane are what it's all about. Every season, stock car racing offers up some of the world's most thrilling competition on wheels. Here are some of the greatest races and most definitive moments in the history of the sport.

Chapter One

The First Organized Stock Car Race
1903

Located about five miles north of Daytona, Ormond Beach is widely considered the birthplace of stock car racing. The wide coastline around Ormond offered three unique and important qualities that made it the best for racing: the beach sloped slightly, making it easy for drivers to handle the cars at top speeds; the tide left a vast expanse of beach open for multiple cars to pass each other; and there was quartz in the sand, making it pack hard enough for the tires to grip.

* Λ *

Speed records were set and broken at Ormond Beach almost every year following the turn of the 20th century, from a once-amazing 68 miles per hour in 1903 to almost 300 miles per hour in 1935. For three days, March 26–28, 1903, seven teams gathered to conduct time trials and try to set a new land speed record, but only two of the vehicles were considered race cars: Alexander Winton's *Bullet* and Ransom E. Olds' *Pirate*.

The event was also a marketing opportunity for car manufacturers and was sponsored by *Automobile Magazine* and the owners of the Ormond Hotel, who were looking to boost room sales. But the event was the brainchild of a marketing genius known as "Senator" William J. Morgan, an English ex-patriot who had carved out a name for himself as a promoter thanks to his mentor, Buffalo Bill Cody, whose Wild West Show had toured the UK and attracted Morgan's attention.

Morgan had read an article in *Automobile Magazine* about speed records being set on the sands of Ormond Beach and visited the area to see if it would be suitable as a host venue for a big moneymaking event. His findings were favorable, and he enlisted the Ormond Hotel owners and the magazine's publishers to back the three-day time trials.

Ransom E. Olds formed his fledgling auto company in 1897, and recognizing that performance could be a powerful sales and marketing tool, he constructed a vehicle to set the land speed record for lightweight cars.

It was Olds' foreman H.T. Thomas who actually piloted the *Pirate* to a 54.38-miles-per-hour record for a lightweight auto. The Winton car was three times heavier and was in a different class altogether. Normally, these cars would never have met in a race, but Morgan's promotional savvy brought the two cars to the beach at the same time. Although it has been widely accepted by historians and racing aficionados that they both departed on their time trial at the same time under a starter's orders, it was the heavier Winton car that started a couple of minutes later. In fact, the cars was not supposed to race each other, just undergo individual time trials, but the promotions-savvy Morgan apparently manipulated the timing of each car's event to create a race situation. And boys being boys with such wonderful big toys, their machismo kicked in, and one driver pushed the other. Before anyone knew it, it was a race—for pride! Although there is no known proof of the fact, it wouldn't be a surprise to learn that Morgan may have had a few bets going on the side and cleaned up.

By the late '30s, stock car racing moved to a banked speedway down the coast at Daytona Beach, but all the greats of early stock car racing competed on the sands of Ormond, from Barney Oldfield and the Stanley brothers of Stanley Steamer days to Eddie Rickenbacker and Sir Malcolm Campbell, whose 5-ton, 30-foot-long *Bluebird V* set speed records in excess of 300 miles per hour.

 FAST FACTS

Canada Hosts NASCAR
The Early '50s

Richard Petty's first race that counts in his 1185 starts actually took place in Toronto, Canada. NASCAR ran two events in Canada during the '50s. The first was held on July 1, 1952, at Stamford Park in Niagara Falls, Ontario. That race was won by Buddy Shuman in a Hudson Hornet. The second race in Canada was run in the summer of 1958 at the Canadian National Exhibition Speedway in Toronto. Lee Petty won the race in an Oldsmobile. Toronto also marked his son Richard's first race in NASCAR's premier series.

Chapter Two

Rapid Roy and Other Good Ol' Boys
Pre-Wold War II

"Ol' Rapid Roy, that stock car boy, he too much to believe…" go the words to a popular '70s Jim Croce song. Very few music fans knew at the time that Rapid Roy Hall was a real person and a star of early stock car racing who started his career as a Georgia moonshine runner. Bootlegging was the start of stock car racing, and Roy was part of a colorful family of drivers, owners and promoters who scratched out a living during the period prior to World War II.

Georgia drivers, car owners and mechanics played a key role in the establishment and early growth of stock car racing. Many fans consider Dawsonville one of the sport's founding home bases, and several of the most popular drivers and influential individuals in the sport's early history emerged from the northern Georgia town.

* * *

Raymond Parks was a native of Dawson County and became a well-known Atlanta liquor store owner who funded several of the popular early racers. In 1938, Parks' cousins Roy Hall and Lloyd Seay, also from Dawson County, were successful moonshine runners and persuaded Parks to front the money for their fledgling racing careers. Atlanta garage owner and mechanic Red Vogt supplied the cousins with the best cars.

Vogt, originally from Washington, DC, quit school by the fifth grade, but at age 16, he was managing a large auto repair shop. During Prohibition, he ran illegal Canadian whiskey from the Canadian border all the way to the White House for three different presidents. Vogt received $100 per carload, a small fortune by the day's standards. He is actually credited with coming up with the name National Association for Stock Car Auto Racing (NASCAR).

Rapid Roy and Seay dominated the stock car racing scene in the Southeast and Midwest during the late '30s and early '40s. But despite playing such an important founding role, neither driver was able to build this into a successful long-term racing career as the U.S. entered the war years. In 1941, Seay argued with his cousin Woodrow Anderson about a shipment of sugar and was fatally shot. Police reports state that the two got into a dispute because Seay purchased the sugar using Anderson's store credit without his knowledge. After World War II ended, Hall was too old to duplicate his pre-war success and faded from the tracks, but not before leaving an indelible impression on those lucky enough to witness his races and disgraces.

Rapid Roy truly was a free spirit who loved the on-the-edge life of a bootlegger turned stock car driver, and he drove each race as if trying to out-run the whiskey "revenuers" instead of his fellow competitors. In 1939, he drove his Ford to victory on a 150-mile dirt track in Salisbury, NC, pushing Bill France back into second. He then took the same car to victory in a 160-mile race on the Daytona Beach road course. In 1945, even though his career was waning, he again outran Bill France in a 75-mile race at Lakewood Speedway. The Lakewood event was the first stock car race after World War II, and Roy blew away the competition. During the 1946 season, Hall arrived in Daytona one evening and cut doughnuts in the street. Complaints from the good folks of the town led to Hall being arrested by the local police. Rapid Roy explained to the officers that he actually wanted to go to jail because the town's hotel rates were way too high.

Parks and Vogt continued to play key roles in stock car racing's early success. In 1947, both men participated in the organizational meetings in Daytona that resulted in the formation of the National Association for Stock Car Auto Racing, headed by Bill France. The Parks-owned and Vogt-prepared cars dominated NASCAR's early races, launching the legendary careers of Red Byron (the 1949 Grand National Champion), Jack Smith, Bob and Fonty Flock and Gober Sosebee, yet another native of Dawsonville, Georgia. Parks retired as a car owner in the early '50s, but Vogt continued working on championship cars for another 10 years.

In May 2002, the history of stock car racing in Georgia came full circle with the opening of Dawsonville's Thunder Road USA motorsports museum, home to the Georgia Racing Hall of Fame. Red Byron, Bill Elliott, Raymond Parks, Tim Flock, Lloyd Seay, Gober Sosebee, Red Vogt and Rapid Roy Hall were all inducted into the Hall of Fame as its inaugural honorees during the museum's dedication ceremony.

Thousands of pieces of donated racing memorabilia, such as car hoods, quarter panels, original artwork, cars used in the early races, license plates, gas station pumps, track signs and photographs, are on display at Thunder Road USA, but one of the most popular exhibits is a real moonshiner's whiskey still. Perhaps the ghosts of Roy and Lloyd are still making their midnight runs from the museum.

 FAST FACTS

Auto Manufacturers
Pull Out of Racing
1957

Stock car racing faced a major crisis in '57 when all of the auto makers withdrew from racing in May after an incident at the Martinsville Speedway. Five people, including a child, were injured by flying debris after a crash. Increased prize monies kept the NASCAR organization afloat until the car manufacturers returned to the sport between 1962 and 1964.

Chapter Three

A Year of Firsts
1949

In December 1948, Bill France founded NASCAR in Daytona Beach, Florida, unifying the small group of sanctioning bodies that sprouted up when Detroit began building new cars after World War II. France decided that his primary audience would be Southern farmers and factory workers, who could relate more to the street-legal, family-style sedans than the funny-looking souped-up "roadsters."

*   *   *

France's association was not the only organization that sanctioned stock car races in the early days. In fact, NASCAR was up against the National Stock Car Racing Association (NSCRA), directed by France's old rival Olin Bruton Smith. Then there was the United Stock Car Racing Association (USCRA), as well as the National

Auto Racing League (NARL), the American Stock Car Racing Association (ASCRA) and the American Automobile Association (AAA). But France was determined that his organization would dominate the stock car world while others focused on the modifieds and roadsters.

North Carolina's Bruton Smith had similar ideas of domination. As the founder of NSCRA, he competed with Bill France and his fledgling group to attract the top drivers, the fastest cars, the most fans and the biggest publicity. France considered Smith such a threat that he decided to attack head-on; he walked straight into Smith's backyard to put on his first official NASCAR-sanctioned 200-lap race. So on a Sunday afternoon in mid-June 1949, the three-quarter-mile dirt track known as the Charlotte Speedway played host to the very first Winston Cup race, which would eventually become the Holy Grail of stock car racing.

Then known as the "Simply Stock" race (later changed in 1950 to the "Grand National" by France), the field of 33 cars included Lincolns, Hudsons, Oldsmobiles, Buicks, Chryslers, Fords, Mercurys and one lone Cadillac.

Although Jim Roper eventually triumphed over Fonty Flock for a $2000 prize purse, the first contest ended in controversy. Original race winner Glen Dunnaway's car, a 1947 Ford, was disqualified for "illegal use of rear springs." Hours after the race, Al Crisler, the chief race inspector for NASCAR, disqualified Dunnaway because the rules clearly prohibited any sort of modification. Car owner Hubert Westmoreland had done a bit of work on the chassis and had spread the rear springs, a favorite trick of old-time bootleggers wanting to increase traction and car handling. The victory spoils were awarded to the Kansas-born Roper, with Fonty Flock, Red Byron, Sam Rice and Tim Flock finishing out the top five. Westmoreland was so infuriated by his driver's disqualification that he sued Bill France and NASCAR, but a North Carolina judge threw the case out. France and NASCAR would win many such judicial battles in the ensuing years.

The first Simply Stock race was an overwhelming hit, with an estimated crowd over 22,000, but France, ever mindful of the taxmen who were watching, promptly readjusted the numbers to reflect an audience of around 13,000. But whatever the actual numbers, France smelled success and quickly scheduled more races in the summer of '49 at Daytona Beach, Florida; Hillsboro, North Carolina; Langhorne, Pennsylvania; Hamburg, New York; Martinsville, Pennsylvania; Pittsburgh,

Pennsylvania; and North Wilkesboro, North Carolina.

Racing was much less formal back then than it is today. Drivers just showed up, and as long as the cars qualified by NASCAR's rules, off they went to the starting grid. In this formative time, young Richard Petty started his stock car career selling race programs in the infield. His father, Lee Petty, raced in a borrowed Buick, and one of the sports' greatest dynasties was born.

That first year, 1949, also marked the first time a woman ever got behind the wheel of a stock car in competition. Driving a Ford owned by her husband, Sara Christian started 13th in that inaugural June race and ran well until she found the going too tiring and handed over her car to Bob Flock, who drove the final 90 laps. She was credited in the official race books with a 14th place finish.

Christian also scored the best finish among any female driver in Winston Cup/Grand National competition history with a fifth place finish at the Heidelburg, Pennsylvania speedway in October that same year.

The Flock family dominated stock car racing throughout the late '40s and early '50s, and sister Ethel Flock-Mobley joined Sara Christian in the history books in 1949, when she participated in a beach race at Daytona. The race really was a family affair, with the Flocks represented in full force by siblings Ethel, Bob, Tim and Fonty. Tim scored the big points for the family that afternoon, taking second place, but Ethel, who drove her husband Charlie's Cadillac, finished a respectable 11th, while Fonty and Bob both fell out early and finished 19th and 22nd respectively. The Daytona beach race was one of only two Grand National races Ethel Flock-Mobley ever drove in.

Despite Christian and Flock-Mobley's early involvement, it took a long time for women to participate en masse in the sport. The first Grand National race with more than one female driver took place the following year at the Hamburg, New York fairgrounds, and featured Louise Smith, a member of the International Motorsports Hall of Fame who participated in 11 races between 1949 and 1950. She raced against Sara Christian and Ann Chester. But it wasn't until the 1977 Fire-cracker 400 at Daytona that multiple female drivers competed again at the Cup level. That race featured Janet Guthrie, Belgian racer Christine Beckers and Italian driver Lella Lombardi.

But unfortunately for women racers, in 1949, as it still is today, stock car racing was a man's world. The 1949 Grand National points champion was Red Byron, followed by Lee Petty in second place and Bob Flock clinching third. Bill Blair, who never won a single race during the first official season, finished fourth in championship points, followed by Fonty Flock and Curtis Turner. Sadly, many of these names have since faded from memory, but these early stars helped shape the sport that now dominates the television broadcast landscape and brought in a larger TV audience than the 2006 Superbowl.

 FAST FACTS

Big Changes Under the Hood
The Mid-'60s

By the mid-'60s, NASCAR's changed its rule that stock cars had to be "stock." Cars became heavily modified for safety in everything except body outline. In 1964, Chrysler introduced the 426-cubic-inch hemispherical engine, generally known simply as the "hemi." The engine was so powerful that Chrysler cars dominated racing. The competition just couldn't keep up, and by the start of the 1965 season, NASCAR banned the hemi, a move that caused Chrysler to pull out of racing yet again to protest Bill France's decision. A sanctioned modified version of the hemi was reintroduced in 1966, and Chrysler returned to stock car racing, this time for good.

Chapter Four

The Southern 500 Is Born
1950

Another important character who played a big part in stock car racing history was Harold Brasington, who brought his dream of building a 1.25-mile paved speedway in his hometown of Darlington, South Carolina, to life.

Joining forces with Bill France, Brasington hosted the first 500-mile race for stock cars, the South's version of the Indianapolis 500, at his new speedway. France was sanctioning races for the second year with his newly formed NASCAR, and he was brought on board to recruit drivers for Brasington's inaugural Southern 500 on Labor Day, 1950. Brasington expected maybe 5000 paying customers to his 9000-seat stadium, but both he and France were amazed when 25,000 people turned up, creating the first traffic jam in Darlington history.

*   *   *

As a 14-year-old boy, Brasington went with his father to the high-banked board track in Charlotte, where he watched in amazement as racers tore around the 1.5-mile track, reaching speeds of 120 miles per hour. The teen knew immediately that racing was his future and spent the rest of his adolescent and young adult years journeying to and from Indianapolis to watch the big boys race at the Indy 500. He was thinking about building a track in his hometown of Darlington.

After he convinced Charlotte businessman J. Sherman Ramsey to turn over a tract of land (formerly a cotton field) off U.S. Highway 151, Brasington soon began construction on a new 1.5-mile paved track that could be used for motorcycles and Indy cars as well as Brasington's beloved stock cars. The whole deal was done on a simple handshake. With additional support from two other business partners, Bob Colvin and Barney Wallace, in late 1949, heavy equipment and cranes were hard at work. Brasington himself often took the controls of bulldozers and grading equipment.

Brasington's blueprints reflected a true oval, but the design had to be altered to satisfy the landowner, Ramsey, who insisted that his nearby minnow pond remain intact. Turns three and four at the west end of the track were narrowed to accommodate the fishing hole.

France originally did not throw his hat in the Darlington ring because he was reluctant to sanction such a short and potentially dangerous race. Brasington pitched the new race to the Central States Racing Association (CSRA) officials, who jumped at the chance to compete against rival France's NASCAR organization. However, after several months of slow ticket sales and a lack of star driver entries, the CSRA decided to withdraw their support. Bill France stepped in after reconsidering the venue's potential to draw crowds and the projected revenues the new track could offer the sport. He brought NASCAR to the table and co-sanctioned the inaugural Southern 500.

At the 1950 race, Long Beach, California native Johnny Mantz drove his black 1950 Plymouth around the lower groove of the track at an average speed of 76 miles per hour, never once changing his tires. France, Alvin Hawkins and Hubert Westmoreland actually owned Mantz's car. During the weeks leading up to race day, the Plymouth had been used as a utility vehicle to haul equipment. On the ninth day of qualifying races, Mantz was able to get the car into racing shape and fitted it with a set of truck tires, which proved more durable than regular car tires. Rules were later put in place to ensure all cars were equipped with uniform sets of tires.

By 1955, the popular Darlington track, known to racing fans as "the granddaddy of them all," was attracting an average high of 75,000 fans to the annual Southern 500, and the crowds keep coming every year. In recent years, the track has been expanded to include Pearson Tower, named after legendary stock car driver David Pearson, a fellow South Carolinian. In addition, the front stretch pit road has been broadened to accommodate a full field of cars, unlike earlier years when there was a bottleneck along the backstretch as cars frantically pitted for refueling.

Harold Brasington's dream has paid off for countless fans and teams who continue to enjoy the thrills and excitement at the Darlington International Raceway. The track, once known as "too tough to tame," continues changing to keep pace with the new 21st century era of stock car racing, but its history remains as a tribute to the drivers and loyal fans who first drove through the Darlington gates over 50 years ago.

Chapter Five

Motor City Celebrates 250 Years
1951

Stock car racing gained some national prominence in 1951 when the Detroit Chamber of Commerce asked Bill France to organize a race as part of the Motor City's 250th anniversary celebration. France chose a one-mile dirt racetrack located on the Michigan State Fairgrounds and planned a 250-mile stock car race—one mile for each year of the city's age. He asked all the auto manufacturers to enter at least one car in the race, and 15 companies signed up.

*   *   *

On August 12, a crowd of 16,500 racing fans lined the track for the Motor City 250, watching 59 cars compete in an exciting hard-fought race with 14 lead changes. The winner was undecided right up until the last lap, when Tommy Thompson drove his 1951 Chrysler across the line to take the flag, outwitting Joe Eubanks in a 1950 Oldsmobile 88.

The Motor City 250 brought about two major breakthroughs for stock car racing: the traditional Southern sport became accepted in the North, and Detroit's auto makers were convinced that stock car's popularity could be good for an auto manufacturer's bottom line. Corporate sponsorships immediately began to boost race profits and winners' purses, and companies like Chevrolet, Ford, and Goodyear began partnerships that have lasted through more than 50 years of stock car racing history. Before these sponsorships, race-car drivers could hardly earn enough in prize money to buy tires, but in the Motor City race, the first, second and third place cars won $5000, $2000 and $1000 respectively. The next seven made a few hundred dollars each, and the remaining 52 entries earned only $25 or $50 for their appearances.

In the new millennium, winners' purses have escalated so much that the top drivers have their racing teams build as many as 12 cars per season at a cost in excess of $100,000 each, all meeting exacting official specifications as well as the driver's personal preferences. Drivers dip into a huge, ever-changing prize pot that includes money from the race purse, TV money, contingency and manufacturer awards and a pro-rated portion of the multi-million-dollar point fund as well as money from the various seasonal plans the car owners have introduced. This is called "total posted awards," but the numbers are fluid. For instance, 2005 Cup champion Tony Stewart could make many thousands of dollars more for placing 15th than the driver who actually wins a given race. It all depends upon individually negotiated driver/owner/sponsor contracts.

In September 1951, an unbelievable field of 82 cars started in the second annual Southern 500 at Darlington. Herb Thomas and Jesse James Taylor took the top two finishes, both driving big, powerful Hudson Hornets. The sheer mass of 82 cars' worth of metal and rubber must have been a real sight in comparison to today's usual 43-car fields. Herb Thomas was one of stock car racing's first superstars, and he was also the first driver to crack the $100,000 career earnings mark. He drove hard and fast and had a "win or bust" philosophy. Between 1952 and 1954, Thomas won 32 races and never finished lower than second in overall point standings. He went on to win 48 Grand National races in 230 starts, and his name remains on the all-time top winners list.

Another major landmark came in November 1951. NASCAR began publishing its own official magazine, *The NASCAR Newsletter*, from its new offices on Peninsular Avenue in Daytona Beach. The first edition consisted of four pages of news, race statistics and driver profiles. These days, the Internet version offers fans the most in-depth detailed coverage of every facet of racing at the click of a mouse, a far cry from the modest little offset-printed newsletter from 1951.

 FAST FACTS

Everybody Is Watching!
1976

The Winston Cup Series took the lead in worldwide motorsports attendance for the first time, with more than 1.4 million spectators in seasonal attendance according to figures published by the Goodyear Tire and Rubber Company. That record has never been broken. Television exposure grew as well.

Chapter Six

The First Daytona 500
1959

With the opening of the Daytona International Speedway in 1959, Bill France risked almost everything he had by building the track in the middle of Florida's swampland some four miles from the beach where he first organized the early races. But the critics and naysayers were proven wrong by the success of what became stock car's most famous annual race.

* * *

Daytona was a massive new speedway with a 2.5-mile track that threw down the gauntlet to car manufacturers to prove whose car was the fastest and had the most powerful engine—and whose car the public would run out to buy on the Monday following the big race (hence the term "Sunday money"). Ford brought in the big Thunderbirds to muscle their way around the track; GM/Pontiac introduced the new Catalina; and Chevrolet trucked in its new '59 Impalas. The entire downtown area of Daytona was draped with car logo banners, bunting and signage, all announcing that stock car racing had come home and was here to stay. All the manufacturers chipped in to raise the prize purses to unprecedented riches, and the entire race week took on the look and feel of a major Hollywood production.

The sparkling new racing palace offered a vast infield where drivers and fans mingled freely. Small portable villages full of race fans sprang up overnight to accommodate the legions of visitors, with barbecues burning and grilling 24 hours a day. Fans set up chairs on top of truck beds and camper van roofs, and they even started trading car parts and other auto-related goods. The infield crowd was pay dirt for race sponsors. Combined with the presence of television and newspaper cameras shooting every inch of the speedway, the opportunity to reach out to new post-war boom-time consumers was like manna from the racing gods.

The first Daytona 500, held on February 22, 1959, received so much hype over the lead-up to race day that even now-legendary newscaster Walter Cronkite came to the track to report on the inaugural event. Every spectator was able to view the entire 2.5-mile track from the grandstand, and no one had ever seen speeds and fierce driver rivalries like the ones showcased on the track that day.

The cars ran so fast that officials could only decide the winner through a photo finish that took over 60 hours to analyze. They determined that Lee Petty's No. 42 Oldsmobile pulled ahead of Johnny Beauchamp's Ford by a fraction of a car length as the checkered flag came down at the end of the race. This finish line photo is one of the most famous images in stock car racing history.

Petty's defeat of Beauchamp was the result of a highly unusual incident. In the final lap of the race, both drivers were passing Joe Weatherly's car, which was well back of the pack and had no chance of winning. Race officials initially announced Beauchamp as the winner when both cars crossed the line, but after they spent three long and agonizing days reviewing amateur film footage and photographs of the finish, the call was overthrown. Lee Petty was declared the official winner of the first Daytona 500.

Driving from 15th position on the starting grid, Petty led only 38 of the race's 200 laps. The race did not have a single caution period to slow the action down. Petty's average speed was 135.5 miles per hour, a blistering pace by the day's standards. His winnings amounted to $19,050, a king's ransom in the late '50s, but a paltry sum compared with the millions today's drivers win.

The payoff for stock car racing as a sport, however, was the unbelievable overnight expansion from a southern-fried party on wheels to a nationwide growth of audience and sponsor interest. Within a month or two of the Daytona race, business consortiums formed and made announcements that they intended to construct other banked raceways, leading to courses springing up in places including Atlanta, Charlotte and California. The '60s brought the new dawn of speed, and as NASA set its eyes skyward towards the moon and beyond, stock car racing set its sights on faster cars, higher ticket sales and broader media coverage.

Inaugural race winner Lee Petty founded one of the most famous racing dynasties in stock car history. The most well-known member of the Petty racing family is Lee's son Richard, who won the Daytona 500 a record seven times and became stock car racing's all-time most-winning driver. Lee Petty was 35 years old before he began racing, but he became one of the sport's pioneers and its first superstar, winning the championship three times. With his sons Richard and Maurice, he founded Petty Enterprises, which became one of NASCAR's most successful racing teams. In 1990, Lee Petty was inducted into the International Motorsports Hall of Fame. He was also elected to the North Carolina Sports Hall of Fame.

FAST FACTS

Television Strikes Gold at Daytona
1979

The 1979 Daytona 500 became the first 500-mile race in history to be telecast live from the green flag to the checkered flag.

Chapter Seven

A Bad Year for Stock Car Drivers
1964

Located on the grounds of the Darlington Speedway in South Carolina, the NMPA Stock Car Hall of Fame and Joe Weatherly Museum features racing memorabilia, historic trophies, imposing racing engines and extreme illegal parts that race officials removed from cars before events. Also on display is the "winningest car," a 1956 Ford convertible belonging to Curtis Turner that racked up 25 wins in one season (the most in stock car racing history). Fans can also see the 1950 Plymouth Johnny Mantz drove all the way from dead last to taking the checkered flag at the very first Southern 500.

But the most interesting aspect of the museum is its name. "Little Joe" Weatherly was originally a champion motorcycle racer who earned three AMA (American Motorcyclist Association) titles between 1946 and 1950 before switching to stock cars. Best known for living his life with joy and gusto, Weatherly was dubbed the "Clown Prince of Stock Car Racing" by his fellow drivers. Following Little Joe's untimely death in a crash at Riverside in 1964, the president of Darlington Raceway suggested the museum to the board of directors, who unanimously approved the concept.

Weatherly was a real character who pulled the wildest pranks on the track, once even driving practice laps dressed head-to-toe in a Peter Pan costume. He was also a party boy and often stayed out on all-night tears, rolling up to the pits just in time to drive in a race. But he could still deliver on the track, notching up 25 victories even though he never completed a full season of races until 1962, when he won seven times in a full card of 52 grueling races. He followed that season with six wins and another championship in 1963.

What was truly amazing, however, was that his team owner couldn't afford to run a car throughout the entire season, so Joe had to beg rides from other car owners. Fortunately, they gave them to him. Weatherly was so tenacious that he actually drove in the '61 Firecracker 250 race using his right leg to bang the gearshift when the gears popped out unexpectedly while operating both the accelerator and brake pedals with his left foot. His hands were busy gripping the wheel as he steered the car in for an impressive sixth place. Not bad for a hitchhiker.

But on January 19th, 1964, the Clown Prince was out of racing forever. The 41-year-old Weatherly was leading in championship points when he arrived at the Riverside Speedway for the fifth race of the '64 season. Qualifying 16th, he was confident about his chances at the same track where he won the 1963 championship title the previous fall.

Many different stories have been told about the cause of the accident. Some observers claimed the transmission in his 1964 Mercury may have malfunctioned. Weatherly pitted, and his crew had hastily traded the clutch and transmission and then sent his No. 8 car back out, even though he was several laps down by then. The *New York Times* speculated the following day that the cause of the crash might have been a stuck accelerator. Later, accounts claim that an inspection of the wreckage found that a brake caliper pin had been dislodged, leaving Weatherly with no brakes as he sped into the track's most treacherous turn.

No matter what story you believe, less than halfway through the 187-lap event, Little Joe slid and lost control as he entered turn six with its dangerous 180-degree curve. His car smashed into the steel retaining wall driver's side first. Some witnesses claimed they saw a puff of blue smoke coming from the Mercury before it careened into the wall. Weatherly had survived combat in World War II, suffering brutal facial wounds, and had made it through many wipe-outs during his motorcycle days, so his devil-may-care attitude may have contributed to his demise—Weatherly didn't like to wear his safety harness or strap down his helmet. The force of the impact jerked Weatherly sideways, and his head slammed against the retaining wall. He was killed instantly.

Because stock car racing was predominantly a Southern sport that still suffered from image problems associated with bootlegging, the death of stock car racing's Clown Prince rated only minimal coverage, which is surprising by today's standards and even NASCAR's popularity at the time. Weatherly's sudden passing warranted less than half a column in the *New York Times* on the Monday morning following the Riverside race; the story was inserted between bowling scores, yacht racing stories and the Monte Carlo rally race results.

*   *   *

For racer Glenn "Fireball" Roberts, the 1964 season also dawned full of promise. The 35-year-old Roberts was fresh off a fifth-place finish in the last season's point standings with four victories in just 20 starts.

Weatherly and Roberts were complete opposites in racing style and character. Early in their careers, Weatherly and Roberts joined Curtis Turner driving for the famed Holman-Moody team. Little Joe and Turner teamed up as buddies on and off the track, doing whatever it took to claim victory—including bumping their competitors and even each other out of the way.

Although he drove for the same team, Roberts had a completely different approach to racing. He was considered one the sport's first "smart" drivers, relying as much on his brains as his accelerator. He maintained peak physical fitness and carefully planned each race by studying other drivers and rating them under the various track conditions and variations. He was also a private person both on and off the track, keeping his personal life to himself. Roberts was also considered NASCAR's first superstar, although he never won a championship. Despite having never won a title, Fireball Roberts is still considered one of the best and most respected drivers in the history of stock car racing. He was named to the organization's list of the Top 50 NASCAR Drivers of All Time and was inducted into the International Motorsports Hall of Fame in 1990.

But the 1964 season didn't start off well for Fireball. During the Daytona 500 on February 21, his car suffered equipment failure, but he managed to take several second place finishes before qualifying for the Memorial Day running of the World 600 in Charlotte. Rumors had circulated that Fireball was thinking of retiring from racing to become spokesman for a national brewing company. But that Memorial Day, he climbed into his No. 22 Ford Galaxie, intent on giving the crowd of over 65,000 a great afternoon of racing—and, of course, taking the checkered flag.

But Roberts had an allergic reaction to flame-retardant chemicals used to treat the drivers' clothing. In the '60s, integrated fire suits had not been developed yet, so drivers suits were soaked in a mixture of chemicals and then hung up to dry before the race. Because of his reaction to the mixture, Fireball Roberts chose not to use flame-retardant on his clothing.

Roberts had qualified 11th in a field of 44 and was in the pack as it settled down on lap seven. As they moved into the backstretch, a chain of events set off one of the most horrendous wrecks in stock car racing history. Junior Johnson's Ford spun out, ramming into the back of Robert's car and sending both them and Ned Jarrett's Ford into a tailspin. Johnson spun away safely onto the grassy apron, but Jarrett and Roberts careened towards the outside wall. Roberts spun backward into the end of the crude cement barrier. On impact, his fuel tank ruptured, and the car rolled over and burst into flames.

Witnesses claimed to have heard Roberts' screams from inside his car. Distraught, Jarrett rushed over to try and save Roberts, but his car was totally engulfed in flames. Risking his own life, Jarrett was able to pull Roberts from the fiery wreck but Roberts had suffered second- and third-degree burns to over 80 percent of his body. Roberts survived for several weeks at Charlotte Memorial Hospital in critical condition, and his health began to improve. But by June 30, Roberts developed pneumonia and sepsis and slipped into a coma, passing away on July 2.

The tragic losses of Weatherly and Roberts, along with Jimmy Pardue's death during a tire test at Daytona Beach the following September, tore the stock car world apart. The sport needed to reassess its safety measures, and the drivers' deaths helped raise awareness of the need for head restraints, better seat belt harnesses and window nets. Finally, after the tragic 1964 season, improved fuel cells were mandated after the introduction of the Firestone RaceSafe fuel tank, and all race cars today use foam-baffled fuel cells to prevent severe gasoline spillage like the one that led to Roberts' death. His death and those of two other drivers at the Indianapolis 500 the same year also led to an increase in research to develop fire-retardant racing suits.

 FAST FACTS

CASCAR Is Established
1981

Founded by president Anthony Novotny, CASCAR is established as Canada's only national stock car racing organization. CASCAR operates the largest and richest racing programs across Canada.

Chapter Eight

Cat and Mouse at the Firecracker 400
1974

During the early to mid '70s, the Organization of Petroleum Exporting Countries (OPEC) oil crisis created problems for auto racing. OPEC refused to export oil to the U.S., Europe and Japan, which inflated American gasoline prices, so the country enforced rationing at the pumps. Many people felt that auto racing wasted precious fuel. To regain public support and show the sport's patriotism, the organizers of the stock car races reduced the number of miles in most races by 10 percent, but Daytona's Firecracker 400 (now known as the Pepsi 400, part of the Nextel Cup Series) remained a 160-lap race (400 miles).

In 1974, strategy and cunning won this nearly three-hour Fourth of July race for legendary driver David "Silver Fox" Pearson. Long-time rival Richard Petty duked it out with Pearson to the checkered flag, but the Silver Fox won with an amazing display of cat-and-mouse strategy that baffled not only Petty, but astonished and confused the fans in the grandstand and even Pearson's own crew chief.

*   *   *

Petty was, without a doubt, the reigning king of stock car racing. By 1974, he had garnered over 100 Grand National/Winston Cup race wins, earning four championships, and he was well on the way to his record seven wins at Daytona. Prior to the race start, Petty had announced loudly how much he wanted to win the Firecracker 400 and had even sent a member of his crew over to Pearson's garage to tell him so. The King (as Petty was known) was not to be denied another victory here—or so he thought.

Pearson, who was no slouch himself, had driven a record-setting season the previous year, winning 11 of his 18 starts in his No. 21 Wood Brothers 1971 Mercury. The Silver Fox had already taken NASCAR's Grand National Division championship in 1966, 1968 and 1969. Pearson started racing in 1952 in a 1940 Ford in South Carolina. His first winnings amounted to the grand sum of $13, which turned out to be a lucky omen. He eventually spent 27 years on the racing circuit, making 574 starts, qualifying in pole position an amazing 113 times (ranking second in all-time pole starts) and tallying 105 wins, 301 top-five finishes and 366 top-10 results. He won 43 races from 1972 to 1979 driving for the famous Wood Brothers team.

Coming through the tri-oval to take the white flag for the final lap, Pearson was leading Petty. As the two men exited the tri-oval, Pearson took his foot off the accelerator completely and drove down to the low groove on the track. Petty passed him, assuming Pearson had run out of gas, and charged ahead to take a substantial two-second, 200-yard lead. But Pearson was just playing possum. He suddenly slammed his foot back on the accelerator and quickly caught up to Petty, drafting behind him to gain momentum, and then edged his car inside to shoot back into the lead as they came off the final turn to win the race. Petty went ballistic, confronting Pearson after the race in the press box. He claimed that Pearson's actions were dangerous and unsportsmanlike. Petty was obviously shaken and embarrassed at being beaten at the post yet again by Pearson's cunning and slick moves.

There were other stars on the track that day. Drivers Buddy Baker, Cale Yarborough and Bobby Allison had all notched many victories and championships, and they were not to be ignored.

The 65,000 fans lining the track got more than their money's worth that race day. While all eyes were on the two leaders, Baker and Yarborough battled it out behind them, finishing in a dead heat to tie for third place—a historic first for a NASCAR race.

The Firecracker 400 netted Pearson a purse of $17,350 and helped him gain third place to Petty's first-place championship in the Winston Cup overall standings. Pearson eventually won over a quarter-million dollars for the season, even though he only had 19 starts compared with Petty's full season of 30 races.

For his efforts, Pearson was inducted into the National Motor Sports Press Association's Hall of Fame at South Carolina's Darlington Raceway in 1991. Two years later, his name was added to the International Motorsports Hall of Fame in Talladega, Alabama, and in 1995, he made it into Charlotte Motor Speedway's Court of Legends. In 1998, he was also named as one of Bristol Motor Speedway's Heroes of Bristol.

FAST FACTS

The End of the King's Reign
1992

Late in 1991, Richard "the King" Petty announced that 1992 would be his final season as a driver. The next year became known as the "Fan Appreciation Tour," and as the season reached its halfway mark, President George Bush Sr. attended the race at Daytona to watch Petty take his No. 7 Ford to the green flag from the outside pole and lead several laps. Unfortunately, Petty was involved in a multi-car wreck in his final race at Atlanta, but he was not injured. Petty was able to get his car back on the track and finish the race. He took a farewell lap to a standing ovation.

Chapter Nine

A Smashing Ending at The Daytona 500
1976

Richard Petty versus David Pearson…again! Every sport has its rivalries. Some are friendly, but others? Not so much. The Petty-Pearson track confrontation is among the most popular stories in stock car racing history, reaching near-mythic proportions. The pair have finished first and second on more occasions than anyone would care to count, and the two rivals are the only drivers in the history of NASCAR to break the 100-wins mark. The final lap of the 1976 Daytona 500 was probably the most dramatic few minutes in racing ever thanks to the daring driving of these two most-venerated icons of the track.

A couple of weeks before the race, Petty had been diagnosed with an ulcer and was laid up in hospital nursing the burning pain in his belly. But on February 15, 1976, it was a pain in his rear bumper that gave him more cause for concern, and that ache still haunts him today.

*   *   *

By 1976, Petty had already logged five Daytona 500 victories, a feat no other driver had even come close to matching. Driving his No. 43 Dodge, Petty again found himself up against his old rival David "Silver Fox" Pearson in his Wood Brothers Mercury. Between them, these two icons of the track had earned seven of the nine championship wins from 1964 through 1972 and had consistently finished first and second in 30 races.

Throughout most of the race, both drivers ran with the lead pack until the 450-mile mark. Pearson and Petty pulled away from the field, and it became apparent to the more than 125,000 fans in the stands that this was going to be a two-man duel to the finish.

With only 22 laps remaining, the green flag stayed out as the gap between the pack and the two front runners grew. Pearson seemed free and clear out front until 13 laps from the finish. Petty suddenly shot past. Startled, Pearson caught up, and they raced bumper to bumper all the way to the white flag. Pearson was sitting almost on top of Petty's rear end, waiting for the split-second perfect time to use the draft behind his opponent's car to slingshot around the leader. Drafting has been a potent and frequently used weapon ever since the early days of stock car racing. Today, it's not unusual to see several vehicles using drafting tactics, including the infamous "bump-draft" where the rear driver bumps the leader, increasing both cars' speed and allowing the rear driver to glide (or draft) faster, giving him the advantage to slingshot past, usually on the lower groove of the track.

Petty and Pearson swapped the lead four times in the final mile, but once they hit the backstretch on the final lap, Pearson got the break he'd been waiting for. He floored the accelerator, and his Mercury flew past Petty along the bottom, taking the lead as they entered the third turn. Suddenly, he hit the banking and drifted up towards the outside wall. Petty slipped his Dodge underneath and was nosing into the lead once again. Going through the fourth turn—bang! Both cars slammed into each other, bobbing and weaving across the track, with Pearson's nose taking a piece of Petty's rear bumper with it. They careened out of control, and Pearson spun dangerously close to the pack of cars a lap down, scraping one of them as they sped past the pit road entrance. In an attempt to avoid the oncoming pack of cars in the rear, Petty feverishly worked the wheel, fishtailing as he fought for control. But it was too little, too late, and he spun several times and slammed into the wall, finally coming to rest in the grassy infield less than 100 feet from the finish line.

In the meantime, Pearson managed to regain control of his vehicle, and after skidding and sliding across the grassy area in front of the pits, the car coughed and spluttered past Petty's wreck to take the checkered flag, creeping across the line at a painful 20 miles per hour.

Petty's crew jumped over the pit wall and surprised everyone by pushing their driver across the finish line. The push from the crew was an illegal move and cost Petty a one-lap penalty. However, both Petty and Pearson had been so far out in front of the rest of the field that Petty still took second-place honours.

ABC Sports had been covering stock car races for some time, and sportscasters Bill Flemming and race legend Jackie Stewart called the Daytona 500 for millions of viewers. As Pearson chugged around to Victory Lane, the announcers' voices could barely be heard above the cheering and hollering of the grandstand crowd, who had been on their feet for the final laps. The entire press box was in chaos as reporters stood on the ledges, craning to see the unbelievable finish. Typewriters flew in all directions, and microphones pulled out of their sockets as the final seconds of Pearson's jaw-dropping crawl to the finish line were broadcast across the country

Richard Petty accepted the blame for wreck immediately after the race, stating his car had gotten loose, but after viewing news footage of the crash, both drivers took responsibility for the incident. Even in the heat of the moment, these longtime volatile opponents had kept their tempers in check. Instead of the anticipated flying fists and four-letter words, both drivers shrugged it off, and the race went into the history books as having one of the most bizarre and heart-pounding finishes of all time.

 FAST FACTS

Two Years of Tragedies
1993–94

On April 1, 1993, defending Winston Cup champion Alan Kulwicki was killed in a plane crash near the Bristol International Raceway. Kulwicki was a real fan favorite who was known for doing things on his own terms. A few months later, 1992 Daytona 500 winner Davey Allison was killed as he attempted to land his helicopter on the infield of the Talladega Superspeedway. He had flown in to see fellow racer Neil Bonnett's son practice at the track.

Instead, Bonnett eventually pulled Allison from the wreckage.

And it was Neil Bonnett who died in the second on-track fatality of the '90s. One of the most successful racers of the '80s, Bonnett chalked up 19 wins throughout the decade. During the 1990 Southern 500 at Darlington, he was involved in a bad crash that forced him to retire from racing. In 1992, Bonnett became a race announcer for CBS and The Nashville Network, but he tried for a racing comeback in July 1993 at the Talladega DieHard 500. The event took place on one of the hottest days ever for a NASCAR race. Going into lap 131, Bonnett's Chevy flipped into the catch fence between the track and the stands. He was relatively uninjured, and after the crash, he even climbed up into the CBS booth to call the rest of the race. Bonnett attempted a full-time comeback in 1994 but died during a practice accident nine days before the Daytona 500.

Chapter Ten

Fists Fly with the Checkered Flag
1979

If you mention "The Fight" to a dyed-in-the-wool stock car racing fan, you'll likely elicit a definite response such as a sharp intake of breath, a knowing nod or a cuss word uttered between gritted teeth. The Fight refers to the brawl between fan favourite Cale Yarborough (the first driver to break the 200-miles-per-hour barrier at Daytona), and brothers Bobby and Donnie Allison that erupted just minutes after the 1979 Daytona 500 ended.

Donnie Allison subsequently received death threats from Yarborough fans, including a letter scratched out in pencil on old-fashioned brown paper stating he'd "better look out for a Coke bottle through your windshield or something like that when you race at Atlanta." But Donnie was not the instigator of The Fight, and it's doubted that he ever threw a punch, but popular legend records it differently.

*   *   *

Thanks to the CBS network, 1979 was the first time the Daytona 500 was televised live from start to finish. Because of poor weather conditions and heavy snow across most of the U.S., the ratings soared far beyond anyone's expectations on race day.

Donnie led most of the way, but as the laps wound down, Yarborough moved up on his bumper and was getting ready to launch one of his famous slingshot moves. The opportunity came on the last lap, and Yarborough made his move on turn two, getting a run on Donnie on the inside. Donnie tried to block Yarborough by bringing his car down the track, but his opening was too far down, and the racers collided. They slid, skidded, then hit each other again, careening into the wall and then bouncing back across the track into the infield. Neither driver won that race. Richard Petty was triumphant this time out, with A.J. Foyt and Darrell Waltrip dueling to the finish line as the television cameras focused on the checkered flag.

For the excited TV network execs, race fans and organizers, the finish would have been thrilling enough, but just as CBS was about to cut away from the race, an unexpected slugfest broke out far away from the bright lights of Victory Lane.

Talk about a heavyweight championship! Luckily, Yarborough and Donnie Allison both escaped the pileup unhurt and were talking heatedly, arguing over who was to blame but not actually coming to blows. Donnie's brother Bobby had driven around the track to check on Donnie's condition. As Bobby sat in his car waiting to see that his brother was okay, Yarborough caught sight of him parked there, strode over to him and then leaned inside Bobby's car and punched him in the gut while he sat there strapped in by his seatbelt.

Bobby had helped his younger brother Donnie get into stock car racing, but unfortunately Bobby also spent much of his own career raging against the racing authorities and the world in general, involving his brother in many of his battles. And on February 18, 1979, he finished a fight that would start the decline of his brother's career.

Somewhat overshadowed by his troubled sibling's career, Donnie's life behind the wheel came to a halt in 1981 during the World 600 at Charlotte when he suffered severe injuries in a crash with Dick Brooks who plowed into his car after Donnie spun out in turn four. After that accident, he drove in only 13 more Winston Cup races. The head injuries Donnie sustained may have made race officials nervous about allowing him into the driver's seat, and his last race was the 1988 Champion Spark Plug 400 at Michigan International Speedway.

But in 1979, everyone who witnessed The Fight agreed that brother Bobby came looking for trouble, and its name was Cale Yarborough. There's a famous Associated Press photo showing Cale and Bobby scuffling with each other, and behind them, you can see Donnie rushing towards them with his helmet in his left hand, coming up behind Bobby. It looks as if Donnie is wading in to join the fight and throw some weight around. Shades of Robby Gordon's helmet hurling incident from the 2005 season? The photo made Donnie look so bad to the public, but it does not reflect a true picture of what happened.

Donnie was actually the only innocent party in The Fight. He was the only one of the three drivers who didn't land a punch, yet he was the one singled out for admonition. Yarborough was already a two-time Daytona 500 winner and would eventually chalk up two more victories. Brother Bobby had previously won the race and would do so twice more. The 1979 race was

Donnie's best kick at the can—he had never won America's Great Race and never would.

Ricky Rudd and Terry Labonte are the only Cup drivers from that race still active on the track 27 years later. The race was Labonte's first Daytona 500 and Rudd's third, but neither knew they'd be part of such a historic moment in stock car racing or what that one race would mean to their sport. Labonte had been sidelined towards the end of the race and watched the incident from where he sat stalled in the backstretch. Rudd had dropped out of the race in the early stages and was on his way home when the brawl broke out. Neither driver has clear memories of the course of events.

To this day, drivers Donnie Allison and Cale Yarborough still debate what happened, perhaps with a little less anger but still with the same enthusiasm. The debate continues over who did what to whom on that famous last lap, and each driver has a different view of that afternoon's events.

In past interviews, Yarborough has said, "He crashed me, it's as simple as that. I was going to pass him and win the race, but he turned left and crashed me. So, hell, I crashed him back. If I wasn't going to get back around, he wasn't either."

Allison counters, "The track was mine until he hit me in the back. He got me loose and sideways, so I came back to get what was mine. He wrecked me, I didn't wreck him."

And so it continues decades later, this "he said–he said" duel of words, but what millions of race fans do agree on is that the 1979 Daytona 500 was one of the single most important and exciting races in the 54-year history of NASCAR. End of debate.

You see, the race did more to move stock car racing into the consciousness of mainstream America than any other. The 1972 introduction of R.J. Reynolds Inc. as a major sponsor was big news. The popularity of Richard Petty in the '60s and '70s was big business as was the opening of several superspeedways in the '60s. But the 1979 Daytona 500 was huge. The media coverage exposed stock car racing to people who had never seen it before and potential sponsors who might not have otherwise given it a look. CBS had taken a big gamble on the live broadcast, since stock car racing had the reputation of being just a sport for "good ol' boys" by most of the country, and in many ways that perception was correct. In 1979, it was still considered a Southern sport that had yet to go national. But that famous Associated Press photo, published in nearly every newspaper in the U.S., and the CBS broadcast, watched by millions, brought stock car racing into almost every American household.

The 1979 Daytona 500 held the TV ratings record for the race until it was finally broken in 2002.

A few days after the race, a reporter called NASCAR president Bill France to ask if he planned to fine the drivers for fighting. "Fine them?" France said, "Hell, boy, I might give them a raise."

"Nobody knew it then, but that was the race that got everything going," said Dick Berggren, who was in the Motor Racing Network announcer's seat on race day. "It was the first 'water cooler race,' the first time people had stood around water coolers on Monday and talked about seeing a race on TV the day before. It took a while—years, maybe—to realize how important it was."

 FAST FACTS

The "Rainbow" Team Wins Big
1994

Only the second youngest driver ever to win the Winston Cup championship, 24-year-old Jeff Gordon drove his multi-colored No. 24 DuPont Chevrolet to victory ahead of race legends Dale Earnhardt, Rusty Wallace and Bill Elliott. Gordon won seven races that season and went on to win the championship in 1997, 1998 and 2001.

Chapter Eleven

Bill Elliott's Million-Dollar Race
1985

On September 1, 1985, at the Darlington Raceway in South Carolina, stock car racing finally came of age. Suddenly, the "good ol' boys" were front-page news everywhere. Even *Sports Illustrated*, known for its disdain of the sport, made the Southern 500's winner and NASCAR's big day its cover story. All of the major television networks spent days running features and interviews on stock car racing, the winning driver and his million-dollar payday.

As the 1984 season came to a close, series sponsor R.J. Reynolds Tobacco announced that it would not only pay the 1985 Winston Cup champion one million dollars, but it would also offer an unprecedented bonus million-dollar paycheck to any driver who won three of the four crown jewels of stock car racing: the Daytona 500 (the most prestigious), the Winston 500 (the fastest), the Coca-Cola World 600 (the longest) and the Southern 500 (NASCAR's old-est race).

The feat had been achieved only twice before, an occurrence so rare that R.J. Reynolds had not budgeted for an actual payout of the prize purse for its Winston Cup sponsorship. However, Bill Elliott, a good ol' boy from Georgia driving a red Thunderbird, had them hastily counting ban-knotes after the more than four-hour-long race left wrecks strewn across the track. Elliott, the driver of the Coors/Melling Ford, was practically the last man standing.

*   *   *

"Awesome Bill from Dawsonville," as Elliott had been nicknamed, began the 1985 season by winning the pole for the first jewel, the Daytona 500. He dominated the race, charging out front for 136 of the 200 laps. Then the Winston 500 at Talladega brought another win, but not without problems. On lap 48, an oil line got loose on Elliott's car, causing him to drop nearly two laps while it was repaired by his swift pit crew. In an impressive display of speed and daring, in less than 100 laps, Elliott made up enough ground to reclaim the lead all the way to the finish line. He got a shot at the million-dollar windfall at the Coca-Cola World 600, but mechanical issues with his car forced him to retire from the race. Then came Darlington and his last shot at the prize in the Southern 500.

Elliott started from the pole and led the first 14 laps. His car was not handling well, so expectations that he would win the race soon disappeared. Dale Earnhardt took charge of the race, taking the lead five times throughout the afternoon over a total of 147 laps. Earnhardt was tailed by Harry Gant in his Skoal Bandit Monte Carlo, who challenged Earnhardt and took over the lead four times, logging 84 laps out front.

Awesome Bill floated back and forth in the lead pack behind Earnhardt and Gant. His car was not set up correctly, and his tires were wearing out quickly. Halfway through the race, the two frontrunners had extended their lead. At around lap 260, Gant took over the front, and Elliott found himself over 19 seconds behind in fourth place trailing Dale Earnhardt and Cale Yarborough, who was also driving a Thunderbird.

By this time, Elliott's left rear tire had blistered and was about to burst, but the fates were kind to Elliott, and on lap 267, Clark Dwyer's car spun out and brought a caution flag that permitted Elliott to hit the pits and make the necessary adjustments to the chassis and the all-important tire changes. When he left pit row, he was able to maintain his track position, but this time, he was only a few seconds behind Gant, and Elliott's car was handling perfectly.

A ninth caution flag came out around lap 294, which allowed a few more minor adjustments, and when Elliott pulled out of the pits, fate once more stepped in to clear the way for him. Harry Gant's car dropped a valve and had to retire from the race. Then on lap 318, Lady Luck not only smiled on Bill, she practically French kissed him.

Earnhardt had run his own brand of race all day, taking risks and handling his car with the skills of a surgeon, weaving in and out of lap traffic and playing lead tag with Gant. But on lap 318, he inexplicably spun out right in front of Elliott. To this day, nobody knows how Elliott maneuvered past "the Intimidator," but as Earnhardt ricocheted off the second-turn wall, Elliott went down low, missing the spinning Monte Carlo by inches. Elliott told reporters after the race that he held his breath, closed his eyes, then floored the accelerator and hoped for the best.

After this near miss, Elliott worked his way around Yarborough. Around lap 324, his battle with Cale Yarborough was won. Cale's No. 28 Hardee's Ford erupted in smoke from a broken power-steering line, spilling fluid all over the track and creating a dangerous black smoke-screen that brought out yet another caution flag. Elliott finally took over the lead, but the final 37 laps saw Yarborough battle back to within a rear bumper's distance of Elliott. But without his power steering, Yarborough's car handled so heavily that he had to use his arms, knees and legs to get it to respond. Elliott took advantage of Yarbrorough's handling problems and stretched out a two-second lead as he crossed the finish line, winning the first Winston Million.

Cale Yarborough placed a heroic second, Geoff Bodine third and Neil Bonnett fourth. The rest of the field of superstars included Bouchard in fifth, followed by Ricky Rudd, Terry Labonte, Benny Parsons, Joe Ruttman and Kyle Petty respectively rounding out the top 10 finishers. But it was Elliott's day to celebrate and Winston's day to show him the money.

In front of a trackside crowd of nearly 70,000, Elliott had brought home his No. 9 Thunderbird with an average race speed of 121 miles per hour over the grueling four-hour spectacle.

Elliott said in later years that the million-dollar race didn't change his life, but it did change the way people viewed stock car racing and gave the sport well-earned new respect. Inside sources close to Elliott confirmed that he actually saw very little of his million-dollar winnings. Team owner Harry Melling received the biggest slice along with Elliott's crew. After taxes, Elliott was left with only around $70,000. And to add further insult to injury, he lost his season-long points lead in the very last race of the season and gave long-time rival Darrell Waltrip the Winston Cup championship. But it was still Bill Elliott who was featured on the cover of *Sports Illustrated*. "Awesome Bill from Dawsonville" also became known as "Million Dollar Bill" as a result of his 11 wins over his record-setting 1985 season.

 FAST FACTS

The Ford Taurus Enters the Race
1998

After Ford mothballed the popular Thunderbird from stock car racing, the Taurus was introduced for competition during NASCAR's 50th anniversary season. Mark Martin drove the Roush Racing Ford Taurus to victory at the Las Vegas Motor Speedway in March, then again in April at Texas Motor Speedway. The new Ford model was a hit.

Chapter Twelve

A Tale of Two Races
1987

Two races carried the Winston name in 1987: the May 3rd Winston 500 run at Talladega, and two weeks later, the Winston run at Charlotte. Both delivered gut-wrenching crashes and both are worthy of mention.

Talladega's Winston 500 gave fans the chance to witness some record-breaking driving and remarkable performances. With a speed of 212.809 miles per hour, Bill Elliott circled the 2.66-mile tri-oval in 44.998 seconds, setting a new NASCAR lap speed record. For the first time in stock car racing history, all of the cars qualified over the 200-miles-per-hour mark.

But the determination and sheer guts of the young rookie in the face of horror most impressed everyone who watched the race that day. Going into the 1987 season, Davey Allison was in contention for Rookie of the Year honors.

Talladega was considered home turf for Allison, and his second-place qualifying time allowed him to share the front row of the starting grid with Bill Elliott to become the first rookie ever to take the outside pole position.

On lap 21, Bobby Allison, Davey's father and fellow Cup series driver, hit a piece of track debris, and his Buick LeSabre took off like a jet, going airborne and barrel-rolling toward the packed grandstands. Fortunately, the car was brought to a halt by the catch fence, preventing any spectator deaths or serious injuries, and Allison Sr. was only slightly hurt. Officials believe that a harmonic balancer broke off his engine and cut up one of the tires.

Crews took over three hours to repair the catch fence and clean the track of debris and oil. On the restart, Bobby's son shook off the horror of the crash. With 10 laps left, he tore up the track as he passed Dale Earnhardt to take the checkered flag and post some of the fastest lap times ever recorded. His No. 28 Texaco Ford was by far the superior car of the day, and he left all the other racers behind, winning with a lead of several seconds.

Following the race, organizers considered mechanical and technical changes that would slow the cars, preventing similar accidents that might endanger the fans as well as the drivers. In 1988, stock car officials imposed a rule requiring cars competing at Talladega and Daytona to run with smaller carburetors and restrictor plates, which limit the amount of air and fuel entering the intake manifolds of the cars, reducing their power and speed. The restrictor plates also increase the time it takes cars to reach their maximum speed, which now can take nearly one full circuit of the track.

*   *   *

May 17th saw the third running of the Winston, which was stock car racing's equivalent of the all-star game. The starting grid included 20 cars piloted by some of the greatest drivers to ever get behind the wheel. Among the stars starting their engines that day were Bill Elliott, Dale Earnhardt, Cale Yarborough, Richard Petty, Darrell Waltrip, Tim Richmond and young Davey Allison, the rookie who had cleaned up at Talladega two weeks earlier.

Dale Earnhardt had practically locked up the Winston Cup Series championship by May that year, building a huge points lead over Bill Elliott and Terry Labonte. His aggressive driving style and bullying tactics had earned him the nick-name "the Intimidator," and he was responsible for leaving a lot of scrap metal on tracks across the country.

As the race got underway at Charlotte, it became clear this would be Bill Elliott's race to lose. He led for two thirds of the race, but as the start of the final 10th lap, Geoff Bodine dashed out in front. Earnhardt quickly moved up on the outside, pulling alongside Elliott and pushing him down onto the track apron. Elliott's car got loose and tapped into Bodine's rear bumper as Elliott drove back up on the first-turn banking, spinning Bodine out. Elliott then pushed up into the high side and Earnhardt darted down low, taking over the lead as the caution flag came out.

As they restarted, Earnhardt had a narrow lead over Elliott and kept blocking every time Elliott tried to pass. Outsmarting the cunning Earnhardt, Elliott faked a move to the high side, and when the Intimidator pushed up to block, Elliott zipped down low going into the fourth turn. Earnhardt managed to block this move too, but caught a fender and spun across the track into the grass. Amazingly, his car quickly righted itself, and he managed to drive back into the lead position—much to Elliott's surprise. After this unbelievable move, the race was unofficially dubbed "The Pass on the Grass."

Going into the backstretch a few laps from the finish line, Elliott came back at Earnhardt, and both cars were forced up to the high side, nearly getting into a wreck at the wall. Two laps later, one of Elliott's tires blew. Bill Elliott's race was over, and Earnhardt had clean air all the way to Victory Lane.

But Elliott was not done with the Intimidator. After the checkered flag, he drove his car right into the rear bumper of Earnhardt's car, jolting him as payback. Earnhardt kept his cool and defended his actions simply with words and a wagging finger. After the race, officials fined both drivers, and Bodine and put all three on probation.

All the speed, the volatile rivalries and the banging about the track at the Charlotte Speedway has assured the 1987 Winston a place of honor in the stock car history books and the memories of the fans.

FAST FACTS

Smoke Rises
1999

Rookie Tony "Smoke" Stewart made an auspicious start to his Winston Cup career, leading an unbelievable 333 laps out of 400 at Richmond International Raceway to take the checkered flag in the Excide Batteries 400.

 FAST FACTS

Frances Passes the Baton to Helton
2000

Mike Helton took over duties as NASCAR President from Bill France Jr. in 2000.

Chapter Thirteen

Allison's Wonderland
1988

Stock car racing changed forever when NASCAR introduced the infamous restrictor plates at the 1988 Daytona 500, but the race is also remembered for a dramatic father-son shoot-out for the checkered flag between Bobby Allison and his son Davey, who would finish first and second respectively. At 50 years old, Bobby became the oldest driver to ever win the Daytona 500, a record that still stands to this day. The 1988 race was also his career third Daytona 500 victory. The race included a spectacular crash at the halfway mark involving "the King," Richard Petty, who was able to walk away gingerly. All the excitement made 1988 one of the greatest Daytona 500 races of all time.

* * *

The lead changed 25 times, with 12 drivers competing for clean air. With restrictor plates on all of the cars, the playing field had been leveled so much that the drivers would be left to rely on drafting skills and cunning strategy to win the coveted trophy. Most of the drivers exhibited respect and caution as they dealt with the new plate handicap, but the bumping, banging and pushing continued. The crowd seemed to hold its collective breath during the prolonged drafting and exciting side-by-side duels.

But on the 106th lap, race favourite Richard Petty tapped bumpers with Phil Barkdoll coming out of turn four, sending Petty's No. 43 skyward, tumbling through six barrel rolls along the outside wall and shredding its rear end as it rolled and was then broadsided by A.J. Foyt. The oncoming pack veered off in every direction trying to avoid getting caught up in the track debris and Petty's mangled vehicle. After taking out Barkdoll and Foyt's cars, Rusty Wallace, Brett Bodine, Eddie Bierschwale and Alan Kulwicki got caught up in the aftermath, but despite the size of the pile-up, there were no serious injuries. Astoundingly, Petty was discharged shortly afterwards from the track emergency centre with just a few minor aches and pains.

Crews took 40 minutes to repair a damaged safety fence after Petty's wild ride. Following the extended caution, Darrell Waltrip took the lead, which he kept until lap 155 when Bobby Allison pulled ahead with Davey close behind him, pushing Waltrip back to third. The trio opened up an impressive 4.16-second lead over the trailing pack. Then on lap 162, Bobby made a pit stop for gas under the green, followed by Davey and most of the remaining field. Waltrip stayed out, hoping to stretch his lead enough to make it nearly impossible for anyone to catch up. Staying out until lap 176, Waltrip extended his lead to 36 seconds, and when he pitted, his over-the-wall crew sent him off with a full tank of gas in only 10 seconds.

Both Allisons had been drafting, decreasing Waltrip's lead exponentially. By the lap 177 mark, none of Waltrip's efforts to stay out front mattered. Another crash brought out the caution flag, and after more pit stops and the lap 183 restart, Phil Parsons took a tenuous lead. Bobby, with Davey in tow, moved ahead, with three other cars including Waltrip's drafting in a line behind. By lap 185, Waltrip's car lost steam and quickly disappeared from the Allisons' rearview mirrors.

With just four laps to go, 13 cars formed a massive drafting line with Bobby out in front. On the last lap, Davey mounted a charge from second place going into the final turn, but he couldn't grab the lead from his father. The Allisons had run a clean race throughout, and with his son's Ford snapping at his Buick's bumper on the final lap, Bobby kept his foot firmly on the accelerator, pulling away to take a two car-length victory. The Allisons pulled off a family victory for the first time since Lee and Richard Petty achieved the same father-son one-two win in July 1960 at the Heidelberg Raceway in Pittsburgh. Rounding out the top five spots were Phil Parsons, Neil Bonnett and Terry Labonte.

In a post-race interview, Davey admitted, "Since I was a kid, I've dreamed about battling to the wire, finishing one-two with my dad. The only difference was, I wanted him to finish second."

Sadly, later in the 1988 season, Bobby suffered serious injuries in a crash at Pocono Raceway. As a result, he experienced severe memory loss and has since said that although he can watch tapes of the 1988 Daytona finish, he can't remember any of the events or emotions of the greatest win of his career with Davey right behind him.

One of the founding members of the "Alabama Gang," Bobby Allison had crowned his 25-year Winston Cup career with the series championship in 1983. He was also the series runner-up five times. The Alabama Gang was the collective nickname of a group of drivers who set up shop and operated out of Hueytown, Alabama (near Birmingham). In the early 1960s, young Bobby Allison left Miami looking for an area that had more opportunities to race and discovered central Alabama, a region dotted with small dirt tracks. Allison was joined by brother Donnie, friend Red Farmer and later by Bobby's son Davey as well as Neil and David Bonnett. Other drivers, most notably Dale Earnhardt, were great friends with the group, and while not Alabama residents, they became associated with the Alabama Gang.

Bobby is tied with old track foe Waltrip for series victories (third all-time) and pole positions (fourth all-time). Bobby is bested only by Richard Petty for most races led (414) and is fourth all-time for most career starts (718). Allison Sr. was named the sport's Most Popular Driver in 1971, 1972, 1973, 1981, 1982 and 1983. In 1993, he was inducted into the International Motorsports Hall of Fame and National Motorsports Press Association's Hall of Fame, and his name was added to the Eastern Motorsports Press Association Hall of Fame the following year.

A sad postscript to the history-making father-son victory in 1988 was the tragic and untimely passing of Davey Allison. On July 12, 1993, Davey was piloting his helicopter on his way to land at Talladega Superspeedway. Something went terribly wrong, and the chopper crashed, critically injuring Davey. The following day, he passed away from his injuries. Prior to his death, Davey had logged 19 victories, and in 1996, he was posthumously inducted into the International Motorsports Hall of Fame.

In October of 2005, superstar Bobby Allison signed on as a spokesperson and commentator for "Reality Racing—The Rookie Challenge," a new reality TV show scheduled to air in early 2006 that gives raw amateurs a shot at a racing contract with a sanctioned NASCAR racing team. As if to memorialize his son Davey, Allison stated to the press, "My whole life has revolved around the passionate pursuit of racing, so I certainly appreciate what it means to have a dream and what it's like to have the opportunity to go for it...at top speeds. I'm glad to have the opportunity to help someone else fulfill their dreams of reaching the winner's circle."

Chapter Fourteen

Short 'n' Sweet in Richmond
1988

Paul Sawyer had been involved in stock car racing long enough to see the writing on the wall. The sadly aging short tracks looked like they might soon become a thing of the past, including his beloved half-mile State Fairgrounds Raceway in Richmond, Virginia. The track's history dated back to a half-mile dirt track known as Strawberry Hill Speedway where the first race took place in 1946, before NASCAR was formed. In 1953, the track was renamed the Atlantic Rural Exposition Fairgrounds, and NASCAR ran the Grand National Series there with Lee Petty scoring the victory. Sawyer and racing star Joe Weatherly purchased the property in 1955, and Sawyer operated the track for the next 45 years.

But when Sawyer took over the helm, stock car racing was still evolving. By the '80s, the Virginia Beach native dreamed of a bigger, more

exciting venue. His small track had been fine
from the '50s into the mid-'80s, but it wouldn't
be able to compete going into the 1990s and
beyond. Sawyer's old track had limited seating
and parking and little concession space. His hospitality facilities were barely adequate, and drivers and crews set up in cramped quarters. The
press corps was banished to even-smaller spaces
around the track with under-serviced communications facilities and tiny work areas. The State
Fairgrounds Raceway just wasn't going to cut it
as it stood, so Sawyer set into action an aggressive upgrade program, much to the amusement
of skeptics who didn't believe there was any
future for the shorter tracks. But after the initial
upgrades and the running of the first race at the
renovated track on September 11, 1988, Sawyer
proved to everyone that short tracks still had
a place in NASCAR.

Sawyer believed that the loyal fans who had
long supported the track deserved better than to
lose the venue, as did the competitors who had
come back and raced there year after year. In the
early '70s, the shorter 100-mile races were being
dropped in favor of 500-milers. If he could
change his track to suit the new style, the longer
races and bigger purses would ensure the Cup
events stayed in Richmond. However, the facilities

would need to be expanded to accommodate fans' longer attendance as well as to support the increased numbers.

Sawyer and his associates made several false starts looking for brand-new track locations in several different areas. But when none of the locations worked out, they decided just to build a new three-quarter-mile track on the same site as their old half-miler.

The proposed new track would allow racing for 400 laps, adding up to 300 miles. The race would fit conveniently into a three-hour TV broadcast schedule, keeping the viewers' attention as well as delivering action and thrills as drivers pushed their cars high around the walls to get as much momentum as possible going into the tight turns.

As the multi-million-dollar makeover began, Sawyer's longtime friend Richard Petty climbed aboard one of the giant bulldozers and began tearing apart the old asphalt. It took an entire month for the buildings to be demolished and carted off, but by mid-April, passersby could see the outline of the new D-shaped track clearly visible in the ground. New 53,000-person capacity grandstands were erected in July, and the asphalt was all laid by the end of August. By the second week of September, everything was in place, and the teams arrived for the Miller High Life 400 on the 11th. Sawyer had taken just six months to transform the tired old track into a sparkling new racing palace.

Although the Sawyer gang knew they could do it, Bill France was less certain that the changes could really be done in time or if they would even work. He was considering booking an alternative venue for the Cup race, but Sawyer was persuasive. He secured the race and the respect of NASCAR for his amazing construction feat.

Paul Sawyer and his partners eventually sold the Richmond International Raceway 11 years later to France and his International Speedway Corporation, a decision that Sawyer's family must surely regret. The track now has 100,000-plus seats and hosts sold-out races throughout the season. The spectacular makeover and successful subsequent expansions prompted the other short tracks at Martinsville and Bristol to quickly follow suit.

If there is a perfect racetrack on earth, many people believe it to be Richmond International Raceway. The three-quarter-mile tri-oval with the 14-degree banking in the turns guarantees fender-to-fender action and produces fast speeds (qualifying laps approach 130-140 miles per hour). Finally, in September 1991, lights were erected around the track and the fall race moved to the evening for the first time. Now, both of the track's Nextel Cup races are run at night.

 FAST FACTS

Gordon Leaves All Challengers In the Dust
2001

With a huge 349-point lead over his nearest rival, Tony Stewart, Jeff Gordon again tasted victory with the Winston Cup Series championship. But for fans and drivers alike, it was a bittersweet ending to a season that started with tragedy when Dale Earnhardt Sr. was fatally injured on the last lap of the February Daytona 500.

Chapter Fifteen

Welcome to the Big Show
1990s

As the century's last decade dawned, stock car racing became even more mainstream as younger, hipper drivers took over from the old guard, although Dale Earnhardt continued his warrior-like dominance on the tracks. His main contenders at the time were youngsters Mark Martin, Ricky Rudd and Rusty Wallace, names that are familiar to many people, even those who aren't stock car racing history buffs.

In 1991, a new television network, TNN (The Nashville Network), took an interest in stock car racing and inked contracts to broadcast five major race events in their predominantly country music video and live concert programming line-up. Their audience was largely the same as NASCAR's. Southern rock and country music was always played at the tracks, so NASCAR and TNN made a perfect fit. Back then, broadcasters cut deals with the individual tracks rather than the governing body, and TNN eventually grabbed every Busch Series race that wasn't already signed to ESPN or one of the other participating networks. Currently, under NASCAR's current broadcasting rights structure, major networks and sports cable channels fight tooth and claw in multi-million-dollar deals. NBC, Fox and SpeedTV are the three major players with broadcast rights in North American and international markets, but in the '90s, a new network like TNN could have a real impact and become a big part of stock car's TV presence.

The 1992 Winston Cup season delivered a sad blow to the sport when Bill France passed away in his sleep at age 82 after a long battle with Alzheimer's disease. Since the late '40s, France had guided stock car racing from its infancy to the huge moneymaking machine of today. He was the visionary, the pilot and the promoter of a sport that just couldn't get any respect for so long, but he hung in there and helped forge the NASCAR organization, which is the envy of other associations and the yardstick by which many other sports governing bodies are now measured.

Despite France's passing, 1992 did have some high points. Richard Petty drove his last race in a season that came to be called his "Fan

Appreciation Tour." Alan Kulwicki took the championship in a quiet, methodical manner, winning by a single lap over Bill Elliott. Perhaps even more importantly in the long-term picture, toy companies and merchandisers suddenly woke up to the fact that racing fans wanted a piece of the action. Die-cast collectibles modeled after all the stars' cars were marketed to fans and snapped up by the millions.

The mid-'90s saw the accidental deaths of several legends, but the decade was also dawn of a new era as Jeff Gordon stormed onto the scene in 1994, at age 21 becoming the youngest driver to win at Daytona. The good-looking kid from California stole the spotlight from the veterans and a hip new youthful look came to NASCAR. Gordon's success and growing media recognition brought new audiences to the tracks, especially young women, who swooned over the bashful driver. Gordon soon became the first real heart-throb of modern stock car racing, and it didn't take long for sponsors to notice his appeal. Everybody wanted a piece of Gordon, but he was careful not to spread himself too thin. He signed a long-term contract to drive for Hendrick Motor Sports, and his major sponsors Dupont and Pepsi signed on for the duration (as did Nicorette in the 2005 season). Gordon learned more than just track skills during the '90s, and he parlayed his business sense into co-ownership deals. He is now Jimmie Johnson's boss and car owner. Johnson takes great pleasure in beating his boss to the checkered flag whenever he can, but the two are always be found congratulating each other on Victory Lane no matter who wins on any given day.

By the end of 1994, track attendance had gone through the roof, with nearly five million people attending the 31 Winston Cup events. Track owners and promoters were forced to expand their existing seating, and construction gangs worked overtime building big new grandstands and facilities to accommodate all the fans, media and merchandisers. By 1995, NASCAR declared stock car racing a "lifestyle" and a "national phenomenon," and cover stories were carried by respected periodicals including *Sports Illustrated* and even *Forbes*. The sports governing body opened offices in New York City and developed a presence on the new worldwide web.

Even Hollywood came calling when legendary action movie moguls Jerry Bruckheimer and Don Simpson produced *Days of Thunder*, starring Tom Cruise and a then-unknown Australian actress named Nicole Kidman. Although Cruise and Kidman's off-camera romance was hot,

NASCAR fans and film audiences stayed cold, and the movie died a miserable death at the box office. Several professional drivers appeared briefly as themselves, including Rusty Wallace, whose career was on a big upswing at the time, but apart from a few live racing shots and some authentic garage and pit scenes, *Days of Thunder* felt too contrived, and stock car fans stayed away in droves. Even today, just mentioning the movie's title to serious race fans can cause uncontrollable laughter and bad jokes.

In 1998, fans marked the 50th anniversary of the formation of NASCAR, and celebrations were held at every track. At Daytona, Earnhardt finally won the crown that had eluded him in his career—the Daytona 500. As he drove his black Chevy on Victory Lane, practically every crew member from every team came over the wall to shake his hand, pat the car and high-five the air out of respect for the great driver.

The decade closed out with newcomer and future two-time Cup champion Tony Stewart winning three races in his rookie year, the most won by a rookie since Dick Hutcherson in 1965. He led a pack of exciting newcomers including Jamie McMurray, Casey Mears, Kasey Kahne, Kurt Busch and younger brother Kyle Busch, all of whom are now drawing in more fans, more sponsors and more media hype than ever before. As the year 2000 dawned, NASCAR had become the second most popular professional sport in North America, besting the National Hockey League, the National Basketball Association and Major League Baseball, with only the National Football League drawing bigger numbers.

 FAST FACTS

One Cup Sponsor Leaves and Another Joins the NASCAR Family
2004

R.J. Reynolds, the tobacco company that sponsored the Winston Cup for many years, was replaced by Nextel, the telecommunications giant, injecting even more sponsorship dollars into stock car racing. Kurt Busch, driving the No. 97 Sharpie Ford, won the inaugural Nextel Cup Series championship

Chapter Sixteen

The Brickyard 400
1994

Until August 1994, America's number-one race, the Indianapolis 500, was the only competition on the hallowed track at the Indianapolis Motor Speedway. But in 1994, NASCAR moved in and a brand new tradition was born. For the first time, a series other than the Indy cars was going to race at the Brickyard. Seeing the potential millions of dollars worth of ticket sales, broadcast rights and corporate sponsorship waiting to be claimed, NASCAR president Bill France Jr. and Indianapolis Motor Speedway president Tony George buried years of hostility and announced in February 1993 that NASCAR would stage regular series races at Indianapolis. But the racing community was not convinced this was a good idea. Many Indy purists feared the integrity of the renowned racetrack would be compromised, but the ever-growing popularity of NASCAR fueled the success of the race.

The Winston Cup Series racers would compete annually in a brand-new race, originally called the Brickyard 400. The title came from the speedway's nickname. The track had been known as the "Brickyard" since 1909, when the surface of the 2.5-mile oval track was constructed using over three million bricks. After many upgrades and repeated resurfacing over the years, the "yard of bricks," a single strip of the original surface that now makes up the start/finish line, is all that remains of that three million.

*   *   *

The first Brickyard 400 was watched by more than 250,000 fans and had all of the fanfare and festivities of its sister Indy race. Film, Broadway and TV star Florence Henderson sang "America the Beautiful," and TV's "Gomer Pyle," Jim Nabors, sang the national anthem. Balloons were released above the crowds, and an air force flyover filled the skies. The race was a sellout—more than 300,000 tickets sold within a few days of the race announcement in the summer of 1993.

After the qualifying heats, Rick Mast emerged as the pole sitter and shared the front of the grid with Dale Earnhardt Sr. Mast became the first driver to lead a lap, but by the end of the race, it was Indiana-born Jeff Gordon, in his sophomore year of NASCAR, who won after leader Ernie Irvan cut a right front tire. Throughout the three-hour race, only six caution flags flew, and the lead changed 21 times among 13 drivers. Out of the total purse of $3.2 million, Gordon took home over $600,000 in prize money.

Though its history is short, the Brickyard 400 is now one of the richest and most prestigious races on the circuit and has become a favorite of drivers and fans alike. In April 2005, the speedway's president, Joe Chitwood, announced that the race was to be renamed the Allstate 400 after inking a multi-million-dollar sponsorship deal with the giant insurance company.

Although the inaugural Brickyard 400 doesn't rank as one of the most thrilling races of all time, its launch is certainly a top-10 moment for stock car racing's history books.

Chapter Seventeen

Labonte Takes the Checkered Flag Sideways
1995

Bristol International Speedway is notorious for big wrecks and exciting finishes. On August 26, 1995, the unforgiving high-banked half-mile track lived up to its reputation. An incredible 15 cautions ate up 106 laps of the 500-lap Goody's 500 in a crash-fest that had Dale Earnhardt, as usual, in the thick of things driving as if he was in a demolition derby.

* * *

The 90-minute rain-delayed start was an omen for the race to come. Many people in the stands were surprised when officials gave the starting orders because the torrential downpour seemed to threaten a full day's delay. Throughout the race, the cars were forced to pit several times to allow the rain to subside and the track to drain and dry. It was no wonder that many of the more volatile characters grew impatient and drove erratically, causing widespread damage and may-hem—the word "carnage" was used to excess in the following day's newspaper reports.

But both the crowd and the teams' spirits brightened just before the long-awaited start was called. The pit crews shook off their tension by lining the top of the pit road wall and doing a giant wave, much to the amusement of the crowds and television cameras. Terry Labonte was designated the race "rabbit" and was sent out on the track to test the surface to ensure there was enough grip for the cars to take to the track. After Labonte successfully ran a lap at full speed, the race was declared a go.

Finally, the field was under starter's orders. Mark Martin and Terry Labonte lined up first in the starting grid, with Earnhardt, the Intimidator himself, right behind. The first few laps saw the drivers fall into a single line with nobody taking any risks on the slick surface. After the track soaking, the drivers needed to be cautious as they worked out their racing groove.

But it only took 31 laps before Earnhardt struck. Rusty Wallace, who had worked his way up to the front pack, took a tap from the Intimi-dator on his rear bumper and went spinning into the wall in front of the flag tower. The first caution flag came out, and Wallace, incensed over the early and unnecessary interference, raced around the track and came up alongside Earnhardt in an effort to return the favor and send a message back to the big black Chevy.

Earnhardt swerved twice, nearly wrecking his car in an effort to avoid Wallace's pressure. After the race, the two nearly came to blows when Wallace fired a water bottle at Earnhardt, hitting the roof of the Intimidator's car close to his head.

Race officials were not going to take any of Earnhardt's guff that day, so before the race was restarted on lap 38, they sent Earnhardt to the back of the pack as a reprimand. The penalty only created an even angrier Intimidator, and the behavior out on the track would go from bad to atrocious.

Lap 51 brought out another caution flag after Brett Bodine smashed his Ford into the wall at the fourth turn. Bodine managed to recover enough for the restart, but only 10 laps later, the poor guy was sent flying back into the wall, this time taking a whack from Bobby Hamilton's Pontiac going into the first turn. Hamilton was "black flagged" and sent to the penalty box to sit out five laps, but Bodine's crew chewed up

42 laps' worth of time trying to repair the damage and get him back in the race.

Jeremy Mayfield found himself out front as the race restarted on lap 66, but less than eight laps later, the rains came down again and so did the yellow flag. Cars slowed down and crawled around the track for 17 laps until officials decided it was safe to attempt a restart...again. But as the race went on, the wrecks started piling up, and the yellow flag kept waving. By the time the caution count had reach seven, Mayfield was spun out on the backstretch after a multi-car crash on lap 234.

Caution number eight came 11 laps later with several more cars crashing. The race finally hit the 300-lap mark, and Earnhardt bullied his way to the front by lap 308, holding the lead through an 11th caution after Ricky Craven smacked into the wall at turn four. But Earnhardt uncharacteristically drifted high, tapping into Derrike Cope's vehicle and leaving a car-width's gap that Dale Jarrett filled, passing swiftly below the No. 8 and taking over the lead.

Jarrett kept the clean air up front through several more cautions (that poor flag man's arm must have been dropping off!), and Earnhardt found himself drifting farther and farther back in the pack. He was forced into the pits twice when a cracked oil cooler started smoking, most likely because of his contact with Cope earlier. But the Intimidator was also able to get a new set of tires that gave him the grip to charge back to try for the lead in the final laps.

When the 15th caution ended, Jarrett was still leading going into the 400th lap, but Terry Labonte's Monte Carlo loomed large in his rearview mirror. Thirty-two laps later, Labonte made a charge on the inside going into the second turn and moved up in front of Jarrett. But Dale Earnhardt was not to be counted out. The determined driver had pushed and shoved his way back into contention. With less than 30 laps left, he'd fought his way to fifth, then on lap 488, Earnhardt pushed Jarrett out of the way and moved into second.

Labonte was looking like a sure thing for the win, but on the last lap, he got hung up behind the race stragglers. Earnhardt closed in for the kill. He sat right on Labonte's rear bumper, drafting and waiting to pounce. Coming out of the fourth and final turn, he tapped Labonte's tail. The next few seconds before taking the checkered flag must have replayed in Labonte's mind over and over again in the years since.

Labonte was trapped behind lapped traffic sitting two-wide, and the leader got boxed in, not able to decide whether to take the high or the low groove around them. But the bump from Earnhardt quickly solved that problem. Labonte hit the gas quickly, trying to avoid hitting the cars in front, but he spun out wildly. With his tires squealing and smoking, he hit one of the lapped cars. Before he knew it, he slid across the finish line sideways before coming to a screeching halt, facing backwards and staring at Earnhardt as he passed—in second place!

The battered but unbeaten No. 5 car sputtered onto Victory Lane with most of its right front end crushed or missing. The team photos taken around the car with the raised Goody's trophy show the No. 5 still smoking and leaking, with a collection of lug nuts, bolts, twisted fender metal and other assorted parts lying on the ground, but Labonte's smile is as wide as the hole in his car's hood.

Chapter Eighteen

Gordon's Big Bonus and Earnhardt's Big Bang
1997

The Winston million-dollar bonus had not been won since 1985 when Bill Elliott's name was written on the check. But not only did Jeff Gordon win the race, he won it for the third straight time and took home the big bonus, too.

But the race also started with a bang (or two) when seven-time Winston Cup Series champion Dale Earnhardt failed to complete a single lap in the Southern 500 at Darlington Raceway after smacking the turn one wall, then hitting the wall again with even greater impact going into turn two. It took Earnhardt two laps' time to get his GM Goodwrench Service Chevrolet back to pit road, where he was pulled from the car and immediately transported to the trackside medical center. Following a preliminary medical examination, Earnhardt was transferred to McLeod Regional Medical Center in nearby Florence, where he received a battery of tests including a CAT scan on his chest, head and abdomen, as well as an EKG and a check for carbon monoxide poisoning. Fortunately, all the tests came back negative, but the doctors kept Earnhardt in the hospital overnight just in case. He didn't remember a thing—not even starting the race.

*   *   *

At just 26 years old, Jeff Gordon had accomplished more in five years than many drivers accomplish in a lifetime of racing. On August 30th, all it took was a 0.144-second margin to carry him to victory ahead of a late-charging Jeff Burton to give Gordon a million reasons to celebrate.

Gordon started seventh in front of the more than 75,000 fans in the stands. The first half of his race was unremarkable, but as the laps ticked over, his Chevrolet was not handling well, and Gordon and his crew chief thought he'd likely finish fourth or fifth at best without adjustments to the car during pit stops. To make things worse, around lap 307, Gordon accelerated going into turn two and slammed into the wall, damaging his car and losing focus for a split second.

Gordon managed to regain control and got the No. 24 Chevy Monte Carlo back in the groove. With 50 laps left, he was out in front, but his lead was cut to 0.22 seconds (approximately three car lengths) ahead of Dale Jarrett and Jeff Burton, who were dueling for the second and third spots. Then, on lap 333, the Pontiac driven by Ward Burton, who was at the back of the pack, spun out of the second turn directly into the path of the three oncoming leaders. Thanks to warnings shouted over the radio from each team's spotters high atop the stands, all three drivers managed to avoid a crash and headed straight for the pits as soon as the caution flag was dropped.

Gordon made it out of the pits in first, but Jarrett was close on his tail. Jeff Burton's crew had to replace a set of lug nuts that had fallen from one of his left-side wheels, and the delay dropped him back into seventh place. When the green flag came out on lap 339, Jarrett was joined by Terry Labonte, Ricky Rudd and Mark Martin, all lined up behind Gordon.

To say the last 28 laps of the race were thrilling and nail-biting would be an understatement. The last few minutes of the 1997 Southern 500 produced some of the tensest, most dramatic racing that fans had witnessed in years. Jarrett dogged Gordon, and with only 10 laps left, Jarrett was nose-to-tail behind the leader. Suddenly, there was Jeff Burton back behind Jarrett's car, pushing his rear bumper in the three-way duel. With three laps to go, Burton brought his car down low alongside Jarrett in the first turn and was able to get by the No. 88 car. Gordon's lead grew ever so slightly, but on the second-to-last lap, his margin disappeared as Burton nosed into his rear bumper.

The No. 4 car had given just about all she had; Gordon's crew had taken the spring rubbers out and put new ones back in, all without losing time or position, and now Gordon had the wheel cranked for all it was worth. He found himself sliding back against the wall, so coming off turn four he pointed the car's nose back down on the track. At the same time, Burton had a run going, and in a split second, he plowed into the rear of Gordon's car, almost lifting the wheels off the tarmac.

The leaders bumped and ground their way around to the first turn, with Burton backing off slightly so as to avoid the otherwise inevitable spinout. Finally, Gordon was able to take the outside line and was first to see the checkered flag.

Earlier in the day, during the drivers' meeting, race officials had diplomatically cautioned racers not to crowd Gordon if he was in contention for the big million-dollar bonus—the great publicity such a win would generate was too valuable for the organization to lose. Burton admitted later that he actually did try to push Gordon into the wall but missed. His statement kept his reputation as an aggressive, competitive driver intact, but at the same time, it appeased race officials and kept him in NASCAR's good books.

The No. 24 DuPont "rainbow team" had its driver splashed across the front pages of all the following day's newspapers and the cover of every sports magazine. Every news and sports broadcaster in the country wanted an interview with the new million-dollar man.

In 1997, Gordon capped off his year with the Winston Cup championship, thanks to 10 victories, one pole result, 22 top-five places and 23 top-ten finishes. He also became the youngest driver ever to win the Dayton 500 and broke the all-time single-season earnings record with over four million dollars in his pocket. The season also pushed his career earnings to $13.7 million. No other driver has earned more than $13 million in his career as quickly as Gordon did.

FAST FACTS

Stock Car Racing Joins Hands Across the Border
2004

NASCAR announced a multi-year operational and marketing agreement with the Canadian Association for Stock Car Auto Racing (CASCAR). NASCAR also formed NASCAR Canada, a partnership with TSN that established a Canadian base of operations in Toronto, as well as NASCAR Mexico, based in Mexico City. These new offices supported local racing and extended the marketing of the sport across the borders north and south of the U.S.

Chapter Nineteen

Earnhardt's Last Victory
2000

Most stock car drivers loathe restrictor plate racing; it creates logjams on the track for cars traveling at 200 miles per hour in packs with little room to move and an even tighter margin for error. Dale Earnhardt's opinion of these races was well known—he hated them. But on October 15, 2000, in the Winston 500 at Talladega Superspeedway, Earnhardt fooled everyone with a spectacular display of come-from-the-back speed to clinch the checkered flag in what was to be his final victory.

Alabama's Talladega Superspeedway is famous for its "big wrecks," and many a driver starts his engine with great trepidation. But on this occasion, the expected big wreck didn't occur, at least not until after Earnhardt crossed the finish line. Many of the cars up behind Earnhardt and the second and third place drivers Kenny Wallace and Joe Nemechek crashed as they crossed the finish line four-wide. It was amazing that nobody was hurt.

*   *   *

Earnhardt was considered the master of drafting. Many drivers joked that "Dale could see the air." This skill enabled him to maneuver his black Chevy from 22nd place up to the front of the pack in the final 10 laps. Earnhardt's comeback triumph, his 76th career win, was nothing less than incredible. With less than a dozen laps left, Earnhardt was not considered a threat to any of the lead drivers, but he tore through traffic to secure a stunning victory, earning the Winston's million-dollar bonus for winning as part of the No Bull 5 program, a special promotion that also awarded a million-dollar prize to a Maryland race fan who had been paired with Earnhardt.

Thanks to drafting help from other drivers, Kenny Wallace in particular, Earnhardt had been bumped into the lead several times. In fact, some of these bumps were so violent that Wallace mused afterwards that by "knocking the hell out of him three or four times" he won the race for Earnhardt. Several drivers had forged a secret pre-race alliance to help each other use drafting to aerodynamically negotiate the track in an effort to offset the restrictor plate handicap. Earnhardt collaborated with Wallace and Nemechek, also driving Chevrolets, and the "team" eventually secured the top three places.

Coming off turn four on Lap 168, Jeff Gordon headed for pit road, and Mark Martin slowed down to follow him but took his foot off the accelerator quicker than Bobby Hamilton anticipated. Hamilton slammed into Martin doing a 360 into the inside pit wall and sent Martin spinning across the grass. Gordon was already driving along pit road when the caution flag came out and was able to get a final load of fuel and head back on the track before anyone else pitted. Ricky Rudd refused new tires and only took on fuel, so he was able to get back on the track in second place behind Gordon, who was closely followed by Dale Earnhardt Jr., Mike Skinner and Bobby Labonte, all of whom had taken two tires on their pit stops.

Dale Earnhardt Jr. took the lead around the high side in the first turn one lap after the restart on lap 174. Terry Labonte came up into second behind him, and Skinner managed to pass Tony Stewart's lapped car to claim third on Lap 180, with Rudd and Andretti joining the leaders. It looked like a safe bet to expect the winner would come out of that pack. Earnhardt Sr. was stuck back in 15th position, and he slipped back further to 18th, but he fought back to 15th position by lap 180. Using bump-drafting assistance from Wallace, he battled through the traffic. Then, with just two laps remaining, Earnhardt threaded through the middle of a three-wide group coming off the fourth turn and suddenly found himself in contention.

Skinner and Andretti were fighting to take the lead when Earnhardt started his push to the front. With just two laps left, Dale Jr. and Mike Skinner scraped each other coming out of the tri-oval section, slowing the pack down enough to allow Dale Sr., Wallace and Nemechek to pull away. As the white flag signaled the final lap, Earnhardt Sr. pulled ahead, with Wallace and Nemechek close behind. Earnhardt held the lead as all three cars crossed the finish line.

As the lead cars slowed after taking the checkered flag, the pack that had been hard on their tails slammed and skidded into each other, sending debris across the track. But everyone was able to get out and walk away with just bruised bodies and egos.

Throughout the race, the lead changed hands 49 times. Jeff Gordon had damaged his No. 24

Chevrolet in the previous day's final practice and had to start at the back of the field in his back-up car, but he had eventually pushed his way through the field to take the lead. Bill Elliott, Hamilton, Wallace and rookies Dale Earnhardt Jr. and Matt Kenseth also tasted clean air up front, and by lap 123, Winston Cup points leader Bobby Labonte had taken over first place, becoming the 19th different leader by that time in the race. Terry Labonte, Ken Schrader and even the 2005 Nextel Champion Tony Stewart took turns out front.

Earnhardt's brilliant late-race performance provided probably the most impressive win from behind since Bill Elliott won the Winston 500 in 1985, when he drove from nearly two laps down under the green flag. Nobody realized at the time, though, that this would be Dale Sr.'s last trip to Victory Lane. The champ would take an unexpected bump a few months later in the spring at Daytona and the sport of stock car racing would lose one of its greatest heroes.

Chapter Twenty

Tragedy at Daytona
2001

The Daytona International Speedway is home base to the heart and soul of stock car racing. Race teams focus a great deal of time and energy on their Daytona cars throughout the winter months between Championship Week in November and the launch of racing season in the spring. The Daytona 500 race is hard fought, and the honor associated with winning is widely celebrated. Going into the 2001 season, Dale Earnhardt was NASCAR's career victory leader although he had only won the Daytona 500 once in 1998.

Earnhardt helped create the fame and success enjoyed by stock car drivers today. The legendary racer won seven Winston Cup championships between 1980 and 1994, and during the '80s and '90s, his dirty driving style and menacing black Chevy made him both a favorite and an adversary with fans, fellow drivers and the media. Ask almost any race fan and he or she will have an opinion on "the Intimidator." Even five years after his untimely and shocking death in the closing lap of the 2001 Daytona 500, heated arguments about his ability, his championship records and his character are likely to break out during infield race weekend parties. Son Dale Jr., a Nextel Cup Series driver himself, now carries the memory of his father with him every time he pulls onto a track.

*   *   *

In 462 starts, Michael Waltrip had never won a points race but on this race weekend, he made up for all his years of coming up empty by taking Daytona's checkered flag. The bittersweet note was that he was driving a car owned by Dale Earnhardt.

After the green flag dropped at the start, fans witnessed three grueling hours of side-by-side racing. With the introduction of a new aerodynamic package, the race offered up 49 lead changes by 14 drivers. The cars stayed in a tight pack that created exciting close-quarter racing. But it also served up a horrendous 19-car crash, highlighted by Tony Stewart's car careening skyward with the engine on fire. Bobby Labonte's car also caught on fire, and the garage area became a junkyard. "There was no getting through it. It was like a wall of cars," said Jeff Gordon. Mike Skinner, Ward Burton and a multitude of other contenders were snarled together in the monumental pile-up.

With only a few laps to go the finish line and a suddenly much smaller field, it became a two-car sprint to the flag. Michael Waltrip and Dale Earnhardt Jr. pulled away from a group that included Earnhardt Sr., Kenny Schrader, Sterling Marlin and Rusty Wallace, who was making a last-chance charge to the front. Many in the stands thought Earnhardt Sr. was getting ready to pounce for one final chance to slingshot past the two leaders and bring the No. 3 home for the win. But to more experienced watchers, it looked like Earnhardt was blocking the other cars from closing in on the two front runners, who were part of his racing team.

The race was almost over, yet the famous black Chevy hadn't pushed its way to the front as expected. Earnhardt Jr. and Waltrip were still out front, and fans were getting impatient for Dale Sr. to make his signature move. Instead, he kept blocking the drivers behind, and his car drifted a little towards the bottom of the track where Sterling Marlin was holding his line going into turn three.

Earnhardt's Chevy suddenly skidded down onto the apron of the track, fishtailing as it slid. Rounding the corner, the car's nose tilted towards the outside wall, and Ken Schrader charged straight into Earnhardt's passenger side. Traveling at approximately 180 miles per hour, the No. 3 then slammed headfirst into the wall at turn four. The crash looked inconsequential, almost routine by track standards, but when the car finally came to rest after sliding down into the infield, there was no movement inside.

Television cameras covering the spectacle had already left the wreck behind to cover Waltrip's victory at the finish line. Waltrip went on to Victory Lane, unaware that his longtime friend and car owner would not be there to share the celebrations.

As Waltrip took his victory lap past the smoking wreckage of Earnhardt's car, track emergency personnel were cutting into the No. 3, trying desperately to save Dale Sr.'s life, but he had apparently died instantly on impact. Moments later, Waltrip enjoyed his victory surrounded by crew and family, while in the infield firefighters were cutting into the wreckage to extract Earnhardt's body.

As Waltrip started the press conference and interview session, he was standing atop a tower overlooking the track, which offered a view of the entire scene. As he looked out over the speedway, he realized the seriousness of the situation and that his victory had come at a painful price.

Dale Beaver, the trackside chaplain for the Winston Cup organization, was hurrying over to Victory Lane to offer congratulations to Waltrip, but he was waylaid with the news that he was needed immediately over at the infield emergency care center. The chaplain accompanied Earnhardt and his family to the local area hospital and was with Earnhardt's wife, Teresa, and son, Dale Jr., when doctors pronounced him dead on arrival.

Dr. Steve Bohannon, emergency medical services director at Daytona International Speedway, responded to the crash and confirmed that the 49-year-old legend was killed instantly. He had suffered life-ending injuries at the time of impact, and there was nothing the emergency workers could do to save him. Dr. Bohannon added that there were no visible signs of trauma to Earnhardt's face after the crash. He went on to say that he felt the fact that Earnhardt was wearing an open-faced helmet did not contribute to his injuries.

NASCAR president Mike Helton made the death announcement at 7:00 that evening to a stunned audience of media, family, friends and fans. "Undoubtedly, this is one of the toughest announcements I've personally had to make," said Helton, whose own motorsports career spanned over 20 years. "After the accident in turn four at the end of the Daytona 500, we've lost Dale Earnhardt."

NASCAR chairman Bill France Jr. added, "NASCAR has lost its greatest driver ever, and I personally have lost a great friend." Fans still waiting for a wreck update at the speedway wept when they heard the announcement.

Neil Bonnett, one of Earnhardt's best friends, had been killed during 1994's practice at Daytona, and three days later, Rodney Orr died in a crash, also in practice. Orr was the last driver killed at the track until Earnhardt. The tragic accident was Earnhardt's second major Daytona wreck in five years. Back in 1997, he had flipped along the backstretch towards the end of the race but was only slightly injured. Earnhardt won the race the following year on his 20th try. Since Daytona's opening in 1959, there had been 26 deaths at the track.

Earnhardt's death had NASCAR's spin doctors working overtime after the deadly 2000 season, when three young up-and-coming track stars were killed in three separate accidents. Busch Series driver Adam Petty, the grandson of stock car great Richard Petty and son of Kyle Petty, was killed at Loudon, New Hampshire, in May. Then in July, Winston Cup driver Kenny Irwin died behind the wheel at the New Hampshire International Speedway, and in October, truck series driver Tony Roper was killed at Texas Motor Speedway.

Five days after the Daytona crash, Bohannon changed his story, claiming that had Earnhardt worn a closed-face helmet like almost every other Winston Cup driver did and accepted the use of the new HANS (head and neck support) device, his life may have been saved. When the HANS device was introduced to the drivers and race officials, Earnhardt was an extremely vocal opponent to its enforced statutory use. He criticized other drivers who wore the device, claiming it was too restrictive and pointless in any case. Ironically, it was later discovered that part of Earnhardt's seat belt had broken, which may also have contributed to Earnhardt's death by allowing his body to move forward and strike his chin on the steering column, resulting in a fracture at the base of his skull. His chest also hit the wheel, which fractured several ribs.

There were two memorial services held for Earnhardt. The family held a private funeral on

February 21, 2001, in Kannapolis, North Carolina, approximately one half-hour outside of Charlotte. It is unconfirmed where, or even if, the racing icon was laid to rest in Kannapolis. The second, public memorial took place the next day.

In the days following, race officials held press conferences offering details of the investigation. Dale Jr. assured fans that he would continue racing and that he didn't blame anyone for his father's death, and stock cars were decorated with a special commemorative Earnhardt sticker.

FAST FACTS

A New Canadian Racing City is Born
2005

Edmonton International Raceway, a quarter-mile asphalt oval located in Wetaskiwin, Alberta, joined the NASCAR Dodge Weekly Series for the 2005 racing season. Edmonton became the third Canadian racetrack to join NASCAR, following the Delaware Speedway in Ontario and the Autodrome St. Eustache in Quebec.

Chapter Twenty-One

Greg Biffle Challenges the Champ
2005

Going into the final race of the 2005 Nextel Cup Series, Tony Stewart was already hammering up a shelf on his trophy wall to accommodate the year's championship statue. It would take every other driver wrecking or the earth opening up to swallow the track to take the crown away from Stewart, but Roush Racing's Greg Biffle got within 35 points of dethroning the champ in one of the most exciting checkered flag duels in Cup history.

Winner of the previous year's Ford 400, Greg Biffle came into the race fourth in total Cup points with Jimmie Johnson and the sport's latest golden boy, Carl Edwards, standing between him and Stewart.

Edwards, Biffle's Roush Racing teammate, started from the pole and led 94 laps. His No. 99 Office Depot Ford Taurus dominated the majority of the race, but he lost pace with the leaders in the later stages. Tony Stewart played it safe throughout most of the race, hanging back with the main pack and just holding his points position to maintain his championship.

*   *   *

By the end of the first 50 laps, Jeff Gordon and Ryan "Rocketman" Newman had swapped the lead several times as contenders Jimmie Johnson and Carl Edwards settled in comfortably behind. Stewart moved up into the top 10 early on, but his Home Depot No. 20 kept getting tight, and he was never in contention for the race win. But he didn't need to worry—he really didn't have to win since he had a 52-point lead in the standings over Jimmie Johnson, who crashed and retired on lap 125, giving him a 40th-place finish. Edwards was 87 points behind and Greg Biffle was 102 behind at the start of the day. As long as Stewart stuck somewhere in the top 20, neither Edwards nor Biffle would be able to make up enough ground to steal the championship title.

As the afternoon wore on, it looked as if Casey Mears, in the No. 41 Target Dodge, would finally get his first career win. By lap 175, Mears took the lead after winning the race off pit road. He stayed in command of the race, with Martin running second and Edwards third, until a caution flag came out for debris on the track on lap 251. Edwards pitted, taking four tires, which left him back in 10th on the restart with 11 laps to go. Mark Martin only took two and came out second behind Dave Blaney's Jack Daniels Chevrolet— Blaney had stayed out on the track. Mears and Biffle were right behind Martin after taking two tires each.

At lap 258, Blaney stretched out his lead, but Martin moved up to challenge him on lap 260. They were driving neck and neck when suddenly Biffle appeared out of nowhere, pushing his No. 16 between the two leads. As one TV race commentator yelled, "It's Biffle…where did he come from?" No one had noticed him working up behind Blaney and Martin, including the two lead drivers, who quickly parted like the Red Sea, not wanting to make contact with the No. 16 and spin out.

By lap 265, Martin appeared to have woken up from Biffle's stunning move and pulled up alongside. In the final laps, the two took turns nosing in front of each other. On the final turn, Biffle was on the outside, almost squeezed into the wall by Martin's No. 6 Viagra Ford. There was barely a hair's breadth between the cars as Biffle took the checkered flag, winning by a margin of only 0.017 seconds—less than a quarter length of a car.

After the race, Biffle commented on his thrilling three-wide pass in the *Charlotte Observer*: "Right when I turned in, I was flat on the throttle, and the thing [car] was stuck to the track. They were sort of holding me up a little bit. I kind of breathed the throttle a little bit, and Blaney slid up and gave me just enough room, barely, to get my car between them. Actually, I just dragged the brake pedal a little bit—I never lifted on the throttle—slowed the car down, and then I let up on the brake pedal to get between them…It was a phenomenal pass. But I just did what I had to do."

But for all the excitement and thrilling driving, the win was anti-climactic for race fans and for Biffle. For the second year in a row, Greg Biffle had to share a celebratory burnout in his Post-It/National Guard Ford Taurus with the night's new Nextel Cup champion. This time around, it was Tony Stewart.

Stewart only needed to run a clean race, so he spent most of the day just outside the top 10 and far away from any possible threats of wrecks or run-ins. He finished the race in 15th place, which was just enough to secure the title over Biffle, who, by winning the race, moved up to within 35 points of Stewart, tying with Jimmie Johnson. But Biffle had six wins to Johnson's four, so he edged out Johnson to claim the Nextel Cup's second-place prize purse.

With this second championship title, Stewart became just the 14th driver in NASCAR history to win more than one championship, joining four-time winner Jeff Gordon as the only active full-time drivers with multiple titles. Gordon brought his No. 24 Dupont Chevrolet home in ninth place at Homestead, securing him the coveted 11th position in Nextel Cup standings and a million-dollar bonus.

It wasn't all business at Homestead, though. The race was also the culmination of a great career as Rusty Wallace drove down the homestretch for the last time, finishing in lucky 13th place. The Ford 400 marked the end of "Rusty's Last Call," as his final season had been dubbed. Wallace retired after a 22-year career that began in 1984 with his first full-time season, when he was named Rookie of the Year. He went on to win the 1989 championship and was twice runner-up in 1993 and 1998. With 55 wins, Wallace is ranked eighth on NASCAR's all-time winners list.

In an interesting turn of events at the end of the 2005 season, NASCAR's team ownership policy was suddenly changed to restrict the number of teams one owner could field. The new rules will have a huge impact on the current multi-car teams, including Jack Roush's driving family. Roush drivers took the first four spots at Homestead: Biffle, Martin, Kenseth and Edwards. In 2006, team owners are limited to four Nextel Cup Series teams per organization in an effort to level the playing field for individual owners such as driver-owner Robby Gordon. Multi-car organizations, including Hendrick Motorsports and Roush Racing, will be able to run a fifth team under a limited schedule, possibly using this car to get a rookie ready for the following season.

The 2006 season promised to be another exciting year for stock car racing fans. Carl Edwards was touted as a future Nextel Cup champion, and perennial "bridesmaid" Biffle was poised to complete his trinity of championships, having already won previous Busch and Truck Series crowns. Kyle Busch, 2005's Rookie of the Year, was on his way to a stellar career alongside brother Kurt, the 2004 Nextel Cup champion, whose "incident" with the local sheriff's office in Phoenix late in the '05 season created messy tabloid fodder. And there is no doubt there will be many more thrills, big wrecks and near misses for years to come as 43 cars hit the race-tracks each weekend with millions of race fans standing and cheering their favourite drivers on to victory.

 FAST FACTS

The Greatest Show on Earth!
2006

In February 2006, television viewership for the Daytona 500 soared to such great numbers that it outscored even the Superbowl. Stock car racing became the second most-watched sport ever, right behind soccer.

Chapter Twenty-Two

Stock Car Racing in Canada

NASCAR's premier series, known today as the Nextel Cup Series, has run two events in Canada. The first race was held on July 1, 1952, in Niagara Falls, Ontario. Buddy Shuman won the event in a Hudson Hornet. The second race was at the Canadian National Exhibition Speedway in Toronto. Driving an Oldsmobile, Lee Petty won the competition that also marked the first race of his son Richard's career.

Many Canadian drivers have participated in the U.S.-based race circuits, including Earl Ross, who was crowned the 1974 Winston Cup Rookie of the Year, and Roy Smith, a four-time NASCAR Grand National Division (West Series) champion. Montrealer Dick Foley also raced in the Winston Cup Series and competed in the first Daytona 500. Back in the '50s, Norman Schihl raced in the now-defunct NASCAR Convertible Division.

Stock cars were raced in Quebec and the Prairie Provinces shortly after World War II but with the vast empty spaces between population centers and poor communications networks, it was difficult to form a regulating body or national organization. Most races were run on flat dirt tracks carved out of farmers' fields, and audiences were made up of families and workers in the rural areas. After a few years, groups of drivers and owners began to organize themselves regionally, and soon PA systems were installed and bleachers constructed along with ticket booths and concession stands.

As early as the 1950s, Canadian tracks held races in most NASCAR divisions—hobby, sportsman and modifieds. Bouvrette Speedway in St. Jerome, Quebec, Drummondville Speedway and Riverside Speedway in Montreal and Fury Speedway in Fabreville have all played host to NASCAR-sanctioned East Series races. The West Series races have been held at Western Speedway in Victoria, BC, Westwood Speedway in Vancouver, BC and Langley Speedway in Langley, BC.

Claude Aubin, owner of the Autodrome St. Eustache, is a popular Quebec racing personality and a well-known figure in the history of stock car racing. Aubin became NASCAR North Series champion in 1978 and raced at many of the U.S. venues throughout his driving career.

The Canadian Association for Stock Car Auto Racing (CASCAR) was established in 1981 as the governing body for amateur and professional stock car racing in Canada. The organization currently boasts the highest level of stock car racing competition in the country, with over 150 member teams. CASCAR sanctions Canada's premier national stock car racing series, the 12-event CASCAR Super Series. They also sanction two other racing series, the CASCAR Power Water Sportsman Series in Ontario and Quebec and the CASCAR Flo-Pro Western Series that runs throughout the Western provinces.

The formation of CASCAR by President Anthony (Tony) Novotny created a progressive national organization that continues to grow. Canada's top teams, drivers, racing facilities, corporate partners and fans all play a part to help the sport to grow north of the 49th parallel.

In 2004, NASCAR, CASCAR and Bell Globemedia's TSN (The Sports Network) inked a deal to form NASCAR Canada, allowing TSN to broadcast 16 of the 37 top-level Nextel Cup Series races and Rogers Sportsnet to air nine Nextel Cup Series races during that same season.

Under this deal, TSN's marketing division (TSN Events) was given exclusive rights to NASCAR's Canadian marketing assets, which it can then offer to Canadian businesses. NASCAR Canada acquired multimedia programs, event marketing and a licensed goods program.

The obvious next step would be for NASCAR to create an official relationship with the Canadian stock car racing series. Racing enthusiasts also hoped that a union like the one proposed would bring about opportunities for Canada to host Nextel Cup Series races, perhaps on a street or road course such as Montreal's Circuit Gilles Villeneuve, which hosts the Canadian Grand Prix Formula One race each year.

The agreement allowed CASCAR competitors access to NASCAR's research and development centre in North Carolina, helping teams and organizers address safety and technical issues. It also gave CASCAR access to NASCAR's promotions and marketing expertise.

Stock car racing continues to gain popularity north of the 49th parallel, even though hockey is still the sport of choice for most Canadians. Sponsors are still looking at statistics for the potential big audience impact these moving billboards represent. More Canadian fans are attending races as well as tuning in their TVs every Sunday throughout the season for the "big race." The proposed expansion into the New York market by NASCAR bodes well for Ontario and Quebec fans.

Young guns such as Michael Gold from Sault Ste. Marie, with his Prince–William-like good looks and pending engineering degree, should bolster CASCAR popularity with both the media and fans. And Canadian female drivers have been kicking some serious wheels! In April 1994, Kelly Williams got her name in the record books when she became the first female driver to win in the then-14-year history of CASCAR racing. In the past 12 years, the Caledon, Ontario resident has forged a career full of racing milestones, and she is now an educator and television personality hosting shows on car care as well as a reality show featuring the worst drivers in the country.

Every week, rumors seem to arise hinting that NASCAR is taking over, buying out or merging with CASCAR. But although a close relationship has been forged, CASCAR appears to maintain its plans for home-grown long-term racing programs in Canada.

FAST FACTS

The Legends

Past drivers who gave us some of the most memorable moments in stock car racing history

Driver	Cars Driven	Years in Cup Racing	Cup Wins	Career Earnings
Bobby Allison	Mercury, Buick, Chevrolet, AMC	1961–1988	85	$7,673,808
Dale Earnhardt	Chevrolet	1975–2001	76	over $40 million
Tim Flock	Hudson, Chrysler, Oldsmobile	1949–1961	39	$109,656
David Pearson	Dodge, Ford & Mercury	1960–1986	105	$2,836,224
Richard Petty	Plymouth, Pontiac	1958–1992	200	$8,514,218
Rusty Wallace	Dodge	1980–2005	55	over $40 million
Darrell Waltrip	Chevrolet	1972–2000	84	over $19 million
Cale Yarborough	Chevrolet & Ford	1957–1988	83	$5,645,887

Chapter Twenty-Three

The Future of Stock Car Racing

You can't move forward with anything until you take care of the past, and stock car racing officials have finally given their blessing to the construction of the NASCAR Hall of Fame in Charlotte, North Carolina, in an early March 2006 press conference that took place in Daytona Beach, Florida.

Officials hope that the state-of-the-art building complex that will house the NASCAR Hall of Fame will capture the spirit of stock car racing, honoring racing icons and paying tribute to all the drivers, crews, team owners and others who have contributed to the growth of the sport as well as those yet to come.

The over 75-million stock car racing fans across North America will finally have a shrine to call their own. Charlotte is set to have one of the greatest halls of fame in the world of sports and entertainment. With such a rich racing heritage in the region, the plans include exhibition space, a great hall and a hall of honor, as well as inter-active entertainment and hospitality venues, retail outlets and a state-of-the-art media center for the industry. The NASCAR Hall of Fame will bring stock car racing's history to life, allowing longtime fans the opportunity to relive the sport's greatest moments and educate and inspire new fans.

Located in Charlotte's city center, the NASCAR Hall of Fame will be developed, designed, and operated by the City of Charlotte and the Char-lotte Regional Visitors Authority, with costs esti-mated at $107.5 million. The facility is expected to open in the spring of 2010. The winning design concept is by the world-renowned archi-tectural firm of Pei Cobb Freed & Partners, which has designed iconic structures such as the Javits Convention Center in New York City, the expanded Louvre in Paris, the Rock and Roll Hall of Fame in Cleveland, Ohio, and the U.S. Holo-caust Memorial Museum in Washington, DC.

Although many commentators and fans thought that Daytona Beach, the generally accepted birthplace of the sport, would eventu-ally win out in the selection process, Charlotte really is the natural fit. Over 80 percent of the

Nextel Cup teams, 70 percent of the Busch Series teams and more than half of the Craftsman Truck teams are based in the region. The future development of the sport is also assured as Charlotte is home to numerous motorsport research and development companies as well as the headquarters of all the "suits": the rules officials, accident investigators, corporate officers and directors of all three big race series. The city is also the home of several universities that offer nationally recognized automotive engineering and motorsports programs.

International expansion is also a hot topic of discussion with both media and fans. Many race teams travel south to Mexico, running an early-season street race in Mexico City. Because of initiatives springing from the organization's current mandate to diversify the sport, the Latino community is embracing stock car racing, and Busch Series team FitzBradshaw is fielding Latino drivers, crews and management. Several drivers have also traveled even further south, all the way down under to Australia. One driver who made the trip was Jeff Gordon, who spent several his early seasons racing there to hone his skills.

Robbie Gordon, one of the few Nextel team owner-drivers, has ventured into even rougher terrain. Gordon drove in the famed Dakar endurance race, where he completed seven stages before pulling out in the eighth and most brutal stage after his customized Hummer finally gave up in the desert sands. The adventurous driver took the heart and soul of stock car racing onto a new continent and used every opportunity he could to tell the media covering the African event about the joys of stock car racing.

With the softening of U.S.–China relations, could stock car racing be next on China's international import list? With such a huge potential audience and economic base combined with the notable Chinese business acumen, we might even see a really Far Eastern division within the next 10 to 15 years.

Women are also making inroads as drivers, valued crew members and management personnel. Many of them have outgrown the traditional office-based roles of secretaries, publicists, timekeepers or statisticians. Stock car's women can now be found in the garage as mechanics, engineers and technicians as well as in the offices. Female sports journalists, race officials and highly competitive drivers are also taking the stage.

With the decline in popularity of the more elitist Formula One races and the recent difficulties in the Indy and Champ circuits, stock car racing is becoming the auto sport for everyone. We can all see ourselves behind the wheel, driving full out to the checkered flag. What fan hasn't heard the cheers of the crowd as we take to Victory Lane in our dreams? As little kids pedaling our homemade go-karts around the vacant lot out back, we all imagined what it would be like to be a Petty or an Allison, an Earnhardt or a Jeff Gordon. More tracks are being planned and developed, taking racing into new areas. Along with stock car racing video games, the new Hall of Fame's fan interactivity, and hand-held track-side mini-cams and radio scanners, every fan can participate and feel like they're part of the action. Gentlemen (and ladies)…start your engines!

FAST FACTS

The Checkered Flag
Drivers who have yet to write
their final chapters

In recent years, fans new to the sport have been drawn in by some of the most thrilling racing in the modern era, thanks to a new breed of drivers skilled in mechanics and engineering who don't shy away from using state-of-the-art technology and sharp business savvy.

Keep your eyes on Tony Stewart and Kurt Busch, who are already Nextel Cup champions. Another legend-in-the-making to watch is Jeff Gordon, who has taken more championships and amassed higher career earnings than any other driver in stock car racing history. Mark Martin is closing out a brilliant driving career at the end of the 2006 season with around $40 million in earnings, but veterans Bill Elliott, Terry and Bobby Labonte, Sterling Marlin and Dale Jarrett are still winning races with no end in sight.

Just coming into their own, next-generation drivers are changing the face of racing once again. Greg Biffle, Kasey Kahne, Kyle Busch, Brian Vickers, Jimmie Johnson, Ryan Newman, Matt Kenseth, Jeremy Mayfield and Dale Earnhardt Jr. are all poised for great long-term careers with many exciting, nail-biting finishes already logged.

As technology improves and speeds increase, there is every chance that we will witness "great moments" every weekend during race season. Stock car racing will have a new set of legends, with many more exciting accounts of big wrecks, near misses and fights to the finish line.

Stock Car Terms and Definitions

Stock car racing has its own language. Here are some of the more common terms used by stock car racers and fans.

Aerodynamics

The way air flows over the surfaces of a race car, over and under the body or through the engine and radiator, and the wake of turbulent air left behind a car as it travels

Air dam

An extension on the front bumper that blocks air as it hits the front of the car. The air dam prevents too much air flowing under the vehicle and reducing its speed. It also plays a big role in keeping the front end stable.

Apron

The paved portion of the racetrack that separates the racing surface from the (usually unpaved) infield. The apron is usually flat in comparison to the racing surface. If a car has a problem, the driver goes there to get out of the way.

Backstretch

The section of the track located on the opposite side of the track from the start/finish line. On an oval track, it is between the second and third turns.

Banking

The angle of a track's racing surface

Blocking

Positioning a car to keep the driver behind from passing

Bubble

A driver who is sitting "on the bubble" is the slowest driver of the top 25 during first-round qualifying. The driver can be knocked off the bubble, meaning bumped out of the field, until second-round qualifying.

CASCAR

Canadian Association for Stock Car Auto Racing, the organization that governs and makes the rules for racing in Canada

Camber

The amount that a tire is tilted from vertical so the tire can touch more of the racing surface

Catch can man

The crew member who stands behind the car on the left side and holds a special container at the end of the car to collect gas that overflows from the tank during refueling

Check valve

A safety valve that prevents fuel spills if the car turns over

Clean air

What the race leader enjoys—nothing in front of the car to create dust, debris or downdraft

Competition Performance Index (CPI)

A formula that evaluates driver performance in the NASCAR Weekly Racing Series
including average finish, number of wins,
driver attendance and the average number
of cars in the field

Contingency programs

Bonus money given for good performance
by companies whose products a driver uses
or whose decals a driver runs on his car in
addition to the usual sponsorship dollars

Crew chief

The leader of the race team who oversees
employees and handles the building and
fine-tuning of a race car. He is responsible
for deciding which changes to make to the
car throughout the race weekend and what
strategies to use on race day.

Dirty air

Turbulence created in the airflow behind
a race car that occurs a little farther back
behind the car than the vacuum cars use to
draft

Displacement

The size of an engine measured in cubic inches, regulated for each racing series. For example, a NASCAR Nextel Cup Series car's engine cannot be larger than 358 cubic inches.

DNF

Did not finish

DNQ

Did not qualify

DNS

Did not start

Downforce

The air pressure and downward force that pushes a car onto the track, causing it to stick on the racing surface. Downforce keeps cars from losing traction at high speeds, especially going through the turns.

Drafting

When drivers take advantage of the aerodynamics of other vehicles in front of them. The first car creates a vacuum that actually pulls along the car behind it. Drivers try to race in single file and share airflow among them. Cars cut through the air much faster together than they do separately.

Drag

The aerodynamic force of resistance that hinders a race car as it moves through air. Drag is caused by air flowing beneath the car and lifting it higher in the air, friction between the car's body and the air molecules, as well as air flowing through the cooling system, ducts in the body and open windows. (Air travels into these openings instead of smoothly sliding over the car.) With less drag, a car can accelerate faster, especially at higher speeds, because the car needs less horsepower to move forward through the air.

Driving on a rail

Slang for a great-handling car that is fast and holding its line perfectly

Five-point seat belts

Five belts that come together at the center of a driver's chest. Each of the belts passes through a steel guide that is welded onto the car's frame. Two belts go over the driver's shoulders, two more come from each side of the seat and another goes between the driver's legs. They are all latched together at a single point, where a quick-release buckle locks them into place.

Flagman

The official who is positioned over the race-track just above the start/finish line. The flagman communicates with the drivers by waving different colored flags.

FLAGS

Flag	Signal	Meaning
Green	Start	Go, the race has started or restarted
Blue/Yellow Stripe	Move Over	A car must yield to a passing car
Yellow	Caution	All drivers must slow down and maintain their position. Drivers are not allowed to pass
Yellow/Two Vertical Red Slashes	Oil On Track	Signals an unsafe surface condition
Black	Pull into Pits	The flagman uses this flag to signal that a driver must get off the track
Red	Stop	All drivers must stop. During a red flag period, no repairs or maintenance of any kind may be performed on the race cars
White	Entering Last Lap	The lead car has one lap to go
Checkered	Race is Finished	The winning car has crossed the finish line

Frontstretch

The straight section of the racetrack between the first and last turns

Fuel cell

The gas tank on the race car

Gas man

The pit crew member who steps over the pit wall carrying a 90-pound, 11-gallon can of gas and fills the gas tank. When the first can empties, he usually gets another can from the second gas man (who doesn't go over the wall), and continues filling the tank.

Getting hung out to dry

Racing slang that means a driver has lost the draft and is losing positions by the split second. To remedy the situation, the driver must get back in line with other cars where the aerodynamics are much more favorable to going fast.

Groove (also known as line)

The path around the track where cars run the fastest and handle the best. The groove of a track can shift several times during a race as conditions change.

HANS device

Head and neck support device that fits over a driver's shoulders, attached to his helmet and seat, preventing whiplash action of the neck and head during a collision

Happy Hour

The final hour of practice before an event usually held in the late afternoon the day before the race

Head protectors

Supports built into a driver's seat to keep his head from moving to the left or right during an accident

Infield

The enclosed area in the middle of the race-track where team garages are located. During race weekends, the infield is usually filled with large transporters, merchandise trailers and driver and fan motor homes.

Inside line

The shortest distance around the track, which on an oval track is usually separated from the infield by the apron. On road courses, it is the line closest to the curbs or walls forming the inner portion of turns.

Inspections

The checks NASCAR officials put cars through to approve the vehicles to race, qualify and practice

Jackman

The pit crew member who positions the jack under a specific spot on each side of the car, pumps the handle of the jack one or two times to lift the car off the ground enough for the tire changers to change the tires and then drops the jack and lowers the car

Junk

Slang for a car that is not running well

Lap

One time around a racetrack. Also refers to when a driver passes a car and is a full lap ahead of that opponent. The driver is then said to have "lapped" that opponent. The driver "laps the field" by lapping every other car in the race.

Lapped traffic

Cars that are not on the lead lap. Many times, these cars are considerably slower than the leaders

Lead lap

The race leader's lap. If the race leader laps a driver, that driver is no longer on the lead lap

Loose (also known as oversteer)

When a driver goes through a turn and the rear end of his car starts to fishtail, making the driver feel as if he is losing control of the car and about to spin out. The rear tires are not sticking well to the track and providing enough traction.

Lug Nuts (or **Lugs**)

The nuts that hold tires in place (a loose lug nut can cause major problems and possible spin-outs)

Marbles

Debris such as sand, pebbles or small pieces of rubber that tend to collect on a track's apron or near the outside wall. Marbles are often blamed by drivers for causing them to lose control.

Modern Era

Period in stock car racing history that began in 1972

NASCAR

National Association for Stock Car Auto Racing, the organization that governs and makes the rules for racing in the U.S.

NASCAR Busch Series, Grand National Division

A lower-level series than the Nextel Cup Series. Many drivers begin their professional racing careers in the Busch Series. Drivers train themselves and hone their driving skills before moving up to Nextel Cup Series. Some drivers stay in this league because there is less pressure to perform.

NASCAR Craftsman Truck Series

The NASCAR Craftsman Truck Series is the newest series, featuring souped-up pickup trucks

NASCAR Nextel All-Star Challenge

NASCAR's Nextel Cup Series version of the all-star game. Only past champions and winning drivers are invited to the Nextel All-Star Challenge, which is one of the richest and most prestigious races each season. There are no points on the line, and the winner's purse is more than $500,000. Formerly known as The Winston, R.J. Reynolds and its Winston brand ended a 33-year-long sponsorship at the end of 2003. Nextel Communications took over title sponsorship for this series beginning in 2004.

NASCAR Nextel Cup Series

The NASCAR Nextel Cup Series is the top-level series and features premier drivers. Formerly known as the Winston Cup Series, R.J. Reynolds and its Winston brand ended a 33-year-long sponsorship at the end of 2003. Nextel Communications took over title sponsorship for this series beginning in 2004.

One-groove racetrack

A racetrack with just a single path around it where cars stick to the track and handle well. If a driver gets out of that path, he could be on a portion of the track where there is not enough grip to keep his car stable, and he could end up in the wall. Some tracks have more than one groove, a high groove and a low groove, meaning cars can run side-by-side or two-wide around the track. Some tracks have no grooves because cars race easily on any part of the track.

Over-the-wall crew

The seven crew members who jump over the pit wall to service a car when it pulls onto pit road

Owner

The owner of the entire team. He or she has a financial stake in the race team, and therefore has final say in hiring everyone who works on the team, from the driver to the crew chief to everyone who prepares the cars for racing. The owner must also secure a sponsor to help pay the bills.

Pit boxes

Assigned pit areas, delineated with yellow lines, for the cars in the race to use during pit stops

Pit crew

A maximum of seven people who are allowed to go over the pit wall and service a car during a pit stop

Pit road

A separate road inside a racetrack that usually runs parallel to a track's frontstretch where cars go when they need gas, tires or repairs

Pit window

An estimate of when the crew thinks the driver will need to make a pit stop to refuel

Pole winner (or pole sitter)

The driver who records the fastest lap during qualifying and is rewarded by starting the race from the inside of the two-car front row. The outside pole winner is the driver who had the second-fastest lap during qualifying. He starts the race from the outside of the front row.

Pucker value

A scary moment out on the racetrack for a driver would have a "high pucker value"

Qualify

Drivers must qualify to participate in a race. This means they must complete one or two full-speed laps around the track and meet established lap times. This weeds out slower or unprepared teams that won't be able to get up to speed on race day. In NASCAR Nextel Cup Series racing, qualifying is normally held on the Friday before Sunday's race.

Race suit

The fireproof suit worn by drivers each and every time they are in the car

Rear spoiler

Metal blade that runs the width of the car atop the back of its trunk. The spoiler regulates air as it flows over a car and helps push the back end of the car down into the track, giving the car more traction and better handling.

Restrictor plate (also known as carburetor restrictor plate)

A thin metal plate with four holes that restricts the flow of air into an engine's carburetor, thus reducing horsepower and speed. The device is used to slow down the race cars at the two superspeedways, Daytona and Talladega.

Road courses

Racetracks with complex configurations of left and right turns at varying angles. Road courses may have elevation changes as well. Sears Point Raceway and Watkins Glen International are the only two NASCAR road courses.

Roll cage

The protective frame of steel surrounding a driver that keeps him safe during an accident because it protects the driver from the impact with another car or the wall if the car flips over. The roll cage consists of roll bars made from steel tubing.

Roof flaps

Rectangular pieces of metal attached to the roof of a car that are designed to lie flat when the car is moving forward, but pop up when a car spins backwards or sideways, helping keep a car from becoming airborne

Rubber

A piece of rubber that is placed between the coils of a spring to increase tension and taken out to decrease tension, changing how a car handles

Rubbing

Incidental contact between cars during a race

Safety tires

A tire within a tire. Both tires are inflated and have separate valve stems. In the event of a blowout or flat tire (typically in the outer tire), the inner tire allows the driver to make it safely to the pit. These tires are generally not used on the two short tracks because of the lower speeds and the proximity of the pits.

Saving tires

When a driver takes it easy through the turns and doesn't run the car too hard, so his tires don't wear out too early

Scuffs

Tires that have been on the car during practice, used for only one or two laps

Setup

The way a car is prepared for qualifying and races, including the suspension package, weight distribution and engine tuning

Show car

Former real race car that has been taken out of rotation for being too old, suffering irreparable damage or just not being suited to the driver. Show cars are used for public display and promotions.

Spotter

Team member who watches a race from on top of the grandstands or press box. His job is to be the driver's second set of eyes, telling the driver where to go on the race-track to avoid an accident or when to pass another car.

Sticker tires

New tires that still have the manufacturer's sticker on them

Sticky

A car that has too much downforce and cannot get up to speed

Stop-and-go penalty

When a driver must come down pit road, stop in his pit box for a moment and then drive down pit road to the racetrack

Sway bars

Parts that alter the amount a car rolls to one side or the other through the turns

Taping a car off

When a crewmember places tape over the grill of the car in order to keep air from entering the radiator and slowing the car down. This is done only during qualifying.

Tearing down

When cars are torn down, teams take apart their engines, but tear downs also can include any part of the car race officials want to examine. The winning team goes through a thorough tear down, meaning it will take apart the engine, the suspension, the power train or whatever else officials want to check out.

Tech

NASCAR slang for a technical inspection

Templates

Individual pieces of metal that conform to the body of a car. They are blueprints of each car make, used to ensure that cars conform to NASCAR specifications.

Tight (also known as **pushing** or **understeer**)

When the front tires don't turn well through the turns because they are losing traction before the rear tires. If driver isn't careful, he or she will end up into the wall.

Tire specialist

Team member who changes the air pressure, measures the wear and monitors the temperature of the tires that teams use during practice, qualifying and races

Track bar (also known as **panhard bar**)

The part of the rear suspension that is attached to the frame on one side and to the axle on the other and keeps the car's rear tires centered within the car's body

Tri-oval

A modified-oval racetrack with five turns instead of just four. Usually the extra turn is located mid-way down the frontstretch.

Victory Lane

A roped-off or fenced-in area located in the infield where drivers, crews, owners, sponsors and families celebrate a victory

Wedge

The amount of weight on the left rear and right front corners of the car. Increasing the weight on any corner of the vehicle affects the weight of the other three corners in direct proportion. Weight adjustments are made by turning "weight jacking screws" mounted on each corner with a ratchet. A typical adjustment for a "loose" car would be to increase the weight of the left rear corner of the vehicle, which decreases the weight of the left front and right rear corners and increases the weight of the right front. A typical adjustment for a "tight" vehicle would be to increase the weight of the right rear corner, which decreases the weight of the right front and left rear and increases the weight of the left front.

Wet

A car that is filled with the maximum amount of fuel, oil and water

Window nets

Screens made of nylon mesh material that cover the driver's side window and keep the driver's arms and head in the car in an accident

Notes On Sources

Race statistics, driver profiles and historical information was gathered from the following sources:

AutoRacing1.com. www.autoracing1.com.

CASCAR Racing. Official CASCAR website. www.cascar.com.

CNN Sports. www.sportsillustrated.cnn.com.

Cup Scene Daily News. www.cupscene.com.

Daily Press. www.Dailypress.com

Editors of NASCAR Scene. *Thunder & Glory*. Chicago: Triumph Books, 2004.

ESPN. www.espn.go.com/auto/nascar/ .

Fielden, Greg & the auto editors of *Consumer Guide*. *NASCAR Chronicle*. Lincolnwood, IL: Publications International, 2004.

Fox Sports. www.foxsports.com.

Golenbock, Peter. *Miracle: Bobby Allison & the Saga of the Alabama Gang*. New York: St Martin's Press, 2006.

Gordon, Jeff & Eubanks, Steve. *Jeff Gordon: Racing Back to the Front – My Memoir*. New York: Atria, 2003.

Hendrick Motorsports. Official Website.
www.hendrickmotorsports.com.

Miller, Timothy & Milton, Steve. *NASCAR Now*.
Richmond Hill, ON: Firefly Books, 2004.

Motorsport.com. www.motorsport.com.

NASCAR.com. Official NASCAR website.
www.nascar.com.

Racing Milestones News.
www.racingmilestones.com.

Penske Racing. Official website.
www.penskeracing.com.

Roush Racing. Official website. www.roushrac-
ing.com.

SpeedTV. www.speedtv.com.

Sports Illustrated. www.si.com.

ThatsRacin.com. www.thatsracin.com.

White, Ben & Kinrade. Nigel *NASCAR Racers:
Today's Top Drivers*. St. Paul, MN: Crestline,
2004.

Glenda J. Fordham

Born in England, raised in the wilds of Western Australia, Glenda J. Fordham continues to lead an exciting life. She's been a comedy club manager, a celebrity minder, tour manager and producer, working with stars like Jim Carrey, Billy Crystal, Jay Leno, Reba McEntire and Vince Gill. But in the last 10 years, she's found a consuming passion for the fast life—stock car racing. She spends her summers glued to the TV watching the Nextel Cup races and comparing racing stats on the drivers and pit crews. She loves the thrill of the race, the powerful cars, the skill of the drivers—and especially the stories behind it all.